Photography
and the Law

BY
GEORGE CHERNOFF
AND
HERSHEL SARBIN

Fifth Edition

AMPHOTO
American Photographic Book Publishing Co., Inc.
NEW YORK

Second Printing, July 1978

Copyright © 1958, 1965, 1967, 1971, 1977 by George Chernoff and Hershel Sarbin

All rights reserved. No part of this book may be reproduced in any form whatsoever without written permission from the publisher. Published in Garden City, New York, by American Photographic Book Publishing Co., Inc.

Library of Congress Catalog Number 77-71217

ISBN 0-8174-2422-9 (softbound)
ISBN 0-8174-2437-7 (hardbound)

Manufactured in the United States of America

CONTENTS

Preface

This Fifth Edition of *Photography and the Law* reflects changes in the law which have occurred since publication of the Fourth Edition. In updating this book its value to photographers and others interested in the subject will be enhanced.

These changes will be especially noticeable in the area of obscenity, copyright and right of privacy portions of this book.

It is virtually impossible for a photographer not to be confronted at times with legal problems that affect practically every phase of his work—from the moment he clicks the shutter of his camera and has to determine whether the subject may be properly photographed, to the time he receives the finished picture and has to decide where and how it can be used.

Regardless of whether he be an amateur or professional, he should have sufficient understanding of the law applicable to photography to enable him to recognize the existence of a legal problem and obtain legal advice or assistance before any damage is done.

Photography is one of the few fields that has not been flooded with books explaining its legal aspects. True, articles have been written from time to time on different subjects relating to the law of photography, but the need has been great for a good book treating all legal aspects under one cover. This book is designed to fill that need. It should be a very valuable part of the photographer's equipment.

THE AUTHORS

Introduction

Through the years during which the authors have written a column on legal problems for *Popular Photography,* our readers have often asked: Where can we find – in one place – the answers to all our questions about the legal aspects of photography? This book represents our attempt to supply a satisfactory answer to that question—to provide the photographer with a basic guide and simple analysis of those areas of the law with which he is most concerned.

In a real sense, any book concerning the law must fall short of the ultimate goal of stating precisely what the law is, for the law cannot be set forth in A B C order as a simple set of rules. It is more complex than that. Moreover, social, political and economic change is accompanied by a continuous refinement and shaping of law to meet current conditions. The reader should bear in mind that any book written for laymen about the law must contain some over-simplification if it is not to be so comprehensive and complex that it becomes useless as a guide. We have tried to organize this book and select our material with this in mind.

The first problem—and one which seems to puzzle many amateur photographers—is: Can I snap the shutter of my camera wherever and whenever I please? Can a policeman stop me from taking a picture of a street brawl? Can the guard at a museum prevent me from using flash? Can I take a picture of a battleship or of a military installation? And since taking the picture seems to be a good beginning, this is where we have started.

From there we have moved, in Chapter 2, to the use one may make of a picture, for this is a problem that should be considered almost simultaneously with the snapping of the shutter. Thus, in Chapter 2 the problem of invasion of privacy is covered. We have also discussed when a photographer must have a model release, and what kind of a release it should be.

In Chapter 3 we have moved to ownership, for many of the problems of use are intertwined with the problem of who owns the picture.

When pictures are started on their way to the processor, and perhaps later to a prospective publisher, another group of problems is encountered. What happens if the processor damages the film? Or if it is lost in transit? How can one protect himself against loss of valuable pictures? And is it possible to prove that a picture has a specific value? This is the subject matter of Chapter 4.

Chapter 5 deals with the nude in photography and the law of obscenity. This problem has two distinct levels. The basic, underlying problem is whether the photograph of a nude may be considered art. Where is the line drawn between obscenity and art? Motion pictures as well as photographs in books and magazines are considered in this area. The second problem—a very practical one—involves the manner in which the Post Office and the processor deal with pictures of nudes.

We have already noted that when a picture is to be published, the law of privacy and the model release assume great importance. Chapters 6 and 7 cover two further problems of publication—copyright and libel. How does the photographer copyright his pictures? At what cost? What is the extent of his protection? When *must* a picture be copyrighted? These, and a host of other questions, are answered in Chapter 6. In the following chapter we deal with problems of libel—problems which generally arise from distortions in the photograph or improper captions.

The use of the photograph as evidence in the courtroom has always been an interesting subject, although most photographers are not directly concerned with its problems. Chapter 8 is an introduction to this subject.

Finally, Chapter 9 covers the subject of the status of photography and the statutes requiring photographers to secure licenses. Whether photography is to be classified as a profession, an art or a trade is often an important question when matters of local and state taxation are involved, and it is well for all photographers to be aware of the efforts which have been made from time to time to require licenses.

The authors feel compelled to state once more that the book is intended as a guide to photographers, not as the source of conclusive answers to all their legal problems. Legal advice must, in the final analysis, be obtained from one's own lawyer.

This is the fifth edition of *Photography and the Law*. The previous editions were so well received by those in the photographic field and by those interested in the law applicable to photography that the authors deemed it worthwhile to bring the book up to date, especially in view of the important changes in certain aspects of the law, notably in the area of obscenity, privacy and copyright.

In the hope that this book will continue to serve as a valuable contribution to the field of photography, we have taken the time and effort to prepare this revised edition.

CHAPTER I

Taking The Picture

A photographer's camera is almost always with him—at home, on the street, in the theatre, or at a museum. And his right to use that camera wherever he may be is essentially unrestrained. Nevertheless, there are a few rules restricting the use of cameras, both as to place and subject matter, which every photographer should know. In reading this chapter it is important for the photographer to distinguish between the right to take a picture and the right to use that picture. This chapter is concerned only with the right to take a picture. The right to use it is covered elsewhere in this book.

One general limitation that always applies to the right to take a picture is that the photographer must not commit a nuisance or interfere with others when taking a picture. With this in mind, let us examine the specific places and subject matter to which restrictions might apply.

Pictures In The Studio

The only restrictions applicable to taking pictures in the studio are those which might apply to any business, and these—such matters as Sunday laws and negligence—are either specifically covered by local ordinance or are matters of general legal knowledge, and are therefore not within the scope of this work. (See pp. 111-115 with respect to license requirements for professional photographers.)

A word of caution should be spoken, however, concerning the application of the rules of negligence to photographic studios. People who come into the studio or into your home, if you are using it for picture-taking purposes, are invitees, and you must provide reasonably safe quarters for them. The requirement is well illustrated by a case in which a child, while being photographed, was severely burned when he came in contact with exposed steam pipes next to the table.

In ruling that damages should be paid for the injury alone, the court declared:*

---

*The numbers following specific references to court cases refer to the list of citations beginning on p. 133.

... the owner and tenant cooperated in creating a condition which any reasonable, prudent person must have known could cause injury. The anticipated use of the room, its ineffective lighting, the harmless appearance of the pipe, its potential capacity to severely burn, if contacted when full of steam, the possibility that young children would be present in the room and come in contact with the pipe, were matters which a reasonable prudent person would have considered.[1]

A word of caution is also in order to photographers taking pictures at weddings and other social functions. Injuries may arise from the placement of their equipment in a manner as to create a hazardous condition or explosion of light bulbs.

Pictures In The Street

Outside of the possibility of an occasional local ordinance restricting the taking of pictures on a public street, the photographer's right to take pictures on public streets and highways is clear, so long as he does not interfere with traffic.

The problem here is actually somewhat the reverse, for there are times when individuals try by physical assault to prevent a photographer from taking a picture. In such instances, the courts have generally stepped in to protect the photographer's right to take pictures in a public place. Some years ago New York State even made it unlawful to injure the apparatus of a news photographer engaged in the pursuit of his occupation in a public place or gathering.[2]

However, in a widely publicized case decided by the Federal Court in New York in 1972 involving Jacqueline Onassis, the right of a photographer to take her picture and her children's in public places was severely restricted. The photographer's conduct constituted harassment, intentional infliction of emotional distress, assault, battery, invasion of privacy and commercial exploitation of the personality of the former president's widow. The U.S. Circuit Court of Appeals, in affirming the lower court's decision, held that the privacy essential to individual dignity and personal liberty underlies the fundamental rights guaranteed in the Bill of Rights under the Constitution. Although the widow of the president was a public figure and thus subject to news coverage, the photographer went far beyond reasonable bounds of news coverage by his constant surveillance, obtrusive and intruding presence. This is an important case discused in greater detail in Chapter 2 dealing with the right of privacy. (Galella v. Onassis)[2a]

In The Theatre, Museum, Or Other Public Places

It seems quite clear that a museum can establish its own rules and regulations for the taking of pictures. Some museums simply prohibit any use of photographic equipment. Others will not allow flash or tripods.

Theatres, sports arenas, or other places of amusement may, if they wish, also restrict the use of cameras.

In another widely publicized case decided in the New York Supreme Court in June 1976, a jury awarded $25,000 in damages to an exclusive New York restaurant against the Columbia Broadcasting System because the network's camera crew entered the restaurant without permission and took pictures. The case stemmed from a CBS news feature on restaurants charged with violation of the New York City's health code. The decision was based on interpretation of the law of trespass as applied to the public media. The camera crew entered the restaurant against the objection of the owner "with cameras rolling" and with a purpose other than using the services of the establishment. While the restaurant had in fact been cited by the health authorities for kitchen equipment violations, it developed that on the day before the trespass, the restaurant had been cleared of all violations by the authorities. The network argued that while it did not know of the lifting of the violations its camera crew still had the right to enter the restaurant and that its conduct was protected by the First Amendment of the Constitution. The attorney for the restaurant saw the significance of the case as an individual's right to privacy as opposed to the privilege of the press to have access to newsworthy events. The judge in a pre-trial decision denying the network's motion to dismiss the trespass charge, held that: "The right to publish does not include the right to enter upon the property of these plaintiffs." The jury's verdict and especially the large amount awarded, is still subject to the review of the trial judge and may also be appealed to a higher court. Nevertheless, it is a significant case on the subject of trespass by photographers especially those engaged in the gathering of news events. (*Le Mistral v. Columbia Broadcasting System*)[2b] Although the restaurant caters to the public, it still is a private place for those entering it with a purpose other than to avail themselves of the services and food offered by it. Therefore, the cases which hold that photographers may take photographs in public places (unless there is some rule or regulation against it) are not inconsistent with this decision.

Photographing Money or Securities

The laws of the United States Government, until a few years ago, made it a criminal act to photograph any "obligation or security of the United States."[3] This included bonds, certificates of indebtedness, coupons and deposit certificates, as well as all kinds of U.S. paper currency. Photographing paper money or other "obligations or securities of the United States" is still restricted, but it is no longer absolutely forbidden.

The law[4] now provides that black and white photographs of such "obligations or securities" may be taken and reproduced for "philatelic, numismatic, educational, historical or newsworthy purposes." This list of purposes is fairly broad, and considerable picture-taking can be fitted within its limits. But the use of such photographs for advertising (except for the "legitimate" advertising of qualified numismatic and philatelic dealers) is specifically forbidden. Color motion pictures, slides and microfilms may also be made for the purposes listed above, but you cannot make prints or other reproductions of these color photographs without special permission from the Secretary of the Treasury. Photographing a *portion* of an obligation or security of the United States is subject to the same restrictions as photographing the *whole*.

As compared with the former harsh law, the present restrictions are more in line with the actual government purpose of preventing counterfeiting. A violation of this more liberal law, however, is *still a criminal offense*. Although a first offender who unwittingly violated the law might expect to be let off with a warning and seizure of the offending photograph, any repetition of the offense would probably meet with drastic action.

Since the specific language of the prohibitory statute speaks of reproductions "in the likeness of" obligations of the United States, it is conceivable that one might photograph paper money so that no part of the money is "in the likeness" of genuine money. The distance of the camera from the object, the particular angle at which the photograph is taken, or the sharpness of focus, might avoid the degree of "likeness" which would constitute a violation of the law. The safe way to avoid a violation, of course, is simply not to photograph obligations or securities of the United States except in the manner and for the purposes which the law permits.

Before 1951 the Federal law prohibited illustrations of coins, but in that year an amendment was adopted which removed the restrictions on photographs and printed illustrations of coins.[5]

The penal laws of some states prohibit or restrict the photographing of stocks, bonds and other securities as well as all instruments for the payment of money.[6]

Postage Stamps

The Federal law places exactly the same restrictions on the photographing of postage stamps, U.S. and foreign, as it does on photographing of money.[7]

The Attorney General of the United States, however, has given an opinion that restrictions on postage stamp illustrations do not apply to demonetized stamps of foreign countries—that is, stamps issued by governments no longer in existence or foreign stamps which are not valid as postage in the country of origin. Such stamps may be photographed and published without restriction as to purpose or use of color.

Miscellaneous

During World War II the President of the United States, acting under his right to declare that certain vital military and naval installations required protection against dissemination of information, ruled out the taking of any photograph of military and naval installations and equipment without obtaining permission of the proper authorities.[8] This power may be invoked at any time, and it is well for photographers to be aware of its broad scope.

The law also says that citizenship certificates may not be the subject of a photograph.[9] Bills of lading are subject to restrictions since they could easily be offered as genuine bills of lading. If one knowingly and with intent to defraud, photographs any bill of lading purporting to represent goods, such action is a misdemeanor.[10]

The Courtroom

One of the most controversial subjects affecting photography to come before the courts in recent years involves the application of the former Canon 35, a rule promulgated by the American Bar Association many years ago, restricting the taking of photographs in the courtroom. Canon 35 has been replaced by a new Canon 3 of the Canons of Judicial Conduct. The new Canon 3, which was adopted in 1975, while it somewhat relaxes the old rule to permit photography and recording of courtroom proceedings for limited purposes, is still restrictive in character. It reads in part:

(7) A judge should prohibit broadcasting, televising, recording, or taking photographs in the courtroom and areas immediately adjacent thereto during sessions of court or recesses between sessions, except that a judge may authorize:
(a) the use of electronic or photographic means for the presentation of evidence, for the perpetuation of a record, or for other purposes of judicial administration;
(b) the broadcasting, televising, recording or photographing of investigative, ceremonial, or naturalization proceedings;
(c) the photographic or electronic recording and reproduction of appropriate court proceedings under the following conditions:
(i) the means of recording will not distract participants or impair the dignity of the proceedings;
(ii) the parties have consented, and the consent to being depicted or recorded has been obtained from each witness appearing in the recording and reproduction;
(iii) the reproduction will not be exhibited until after the proceeding has been concluded and all direct appeals have been exhausted; and
(iv) the reproduction will be exhibited only for instructional purposes in educational institutions.

Commentary: Temperate conduct of judicial proceedings is essential to
the fair administration of justice. The recording and reproduction of a proceeding should not distort or dramatize the proceeding.

The above restriction is still difficult to understand. There was a time,
indeed, when the taking of photographs in a courtroom could well be said to
create a disturbing influence. Times have changed, however. Today the camera is a much more unobtrusive recorder than it was when the old Canon 35
came into being many years ago.

During the course of an investigation of New York State trotting tracks
some years ago,[11] a newspaper photographer was ejected from the hearing
room when it was discovered that he was taking pictures with a concealed
35mm camera. He had been taking the pictures for two and one half days
without affecting the decorum of the courtroom. Despite the fact that he had
taken over 30 pictures of political figures as they were testifying, no one had
noticed the camera work.

In the face of such evidence it is difficult for us, and for photographers
generally, to understand the continued vitality of the restriction. Much of the
difficulty, especially in recent years, arises from the fact that justification for
the restriction has so often centered on the courtroom disturbance which can
be caused by television broadcasting, without sufficient separate consideration being given to photography as such.

One interesting case involving the old Canon 35 took place in Cleveland, Ohio, when three staff members of *The Cleveland Press* were convicted
of contempt of court for taking a picture at the arraignment of a prisoner
charged with embezzlement. The judge had told newsmen that no pictures
were to be taken, and the attorney for the defendant quoted the judge as saying, ". . . the ban had been imposed because otherwise he would be disci-
plined by the Cleveland Bar Association."

The newspaper's position was well stated by Mr. Louis B. Seltzer, editor of the *Press,* who said:

It is our basic argument, apart from the direct issue involved, that photographic science has made picture taking in a courtroom beyond the claim
that it distracts or intrudes on the proceedings in a courtroom, and is
essentially no different than a reporter covering a trial with his pencil and
pad.
    It is the further contention that under a broad interpretation of the
constitutional guaranty of a free press in this democracy that the people's
right to know endows the free press not only with ears to write but eyes
to illustrate modern court proceedings.

Mr. Seltzer's argument did not prevail, however, and the Appellate
Court in Ohio supported the judge's ruling. The Court said in part:

The rules of courtroom conduct must be such as to remove it from the
distractions and disturbances of the market place, and to maintain as

nearly as possible an atmosphere conducive to profound and undisturbed deliberation. . . . The flashlight inevitably startles those nearby when used without notice. Its use is not conducive to sustained mental effort. If a photographer can take one picture he can take two or a dozen.[12]

In reaching its decision the Court cited a Supreme Court case which gave the State and Federal Courts "the power to protect themselves from disorders and disturbances in the Courtroom."

In many states, Canon 3 is strictly observed throughout the state, on occasion even being extended to local rules forbidding the taking of photographs in courtroom corridors, or even on the courthouse steps. Generally, taking photographs outside the courthouse is permitted. In some states, Texas for example, the observance of Canon 3 depends on the discretion of the individual judge. Thus, for example, Judge Joe B. Brown permitted *television cameras* in the courtroom when the jury returned its verdict in the Jack Ruby trial in Dallas, but did not permit television *broadcasting* or the taking of still photographs during the actual trial.[13] The Alabama Supreme Court in 1974 adopted a rule allowing television, radio broadcasting and still photography in trials. Colorado permits such coverage. However, the Alabama coverage is discretionary with each court, and in both Alabama and Colorado no witness or juror can be photographed or broadcast over his objection. In New York, by statute, Sec. 52, Civil Rights Law, the taking of moving pictures, televising and broadcasting are forbidden in the courtroom.

Although a few words offensive to photographers were removed from the former Canon 35 as replaced by new Canon 3, it seems to us that over recent years there has been a net loss rather than a net gain to photographers in this connection. Because of the increasing number of states in which there is a statewide rule forbidding any picture taking in any courtroom, the judge is left without discretion to grant permission to a photographer to take pictures except to the extent previously indicated.

Despite the universally severe criticism of the restriction among photographers, we have always noted in discussing the subject with them that they recognize the inherent right of a judge to control the conduct of a trial over which he is presiding, and the necessity of maintaining order in the courtroom. We believe that a judge should be considered competent to do this, and that he should not be compelled to forbid courtroom photography in situations where he does not believe that courtroom decorum would be disturbed.

CHAPTER II

Right Of Privacy

Every photographer who plans to sell, publish or exhibit his pictures must acquire some knowledge concerning the law of privacy and model releases. In this chapter it is our purpose to show you when and under what circumstances you will need a model release, and when you will be reasonably safe without one.

Whenever a photographer sells or exhibits a picture of a living person[1] he runs the risk of being sued for invasion of the right of privacy. In fact, the greatest number of lawsuits brought against photographers today is in this area. What is the right of privacy? Generally, the courts have said that it is the right of a person to be let alone, to be free from undeserved and undesired publicity. It has also been described as the right to live one's life in seclusion, without being subjected to unwarranted publicity.

This does not mean that the mere taking of a person's picture is of itself necessarily an invasion of privacy. Obviously, the public has a right to many types of knowledge that would be cut off if the definition we have used were taken too literally. In the years since the right of privacy was first recognized, the courts of the land have attempted to strike a proper balance between the individual's right to be let alone and the public's broad right to knowledge and information.

In attempting to strike this balance, the courts and state legislatures have uniformly looked to the use to which a picture or a person's name was put. Some states have said the prohibited use was one "for advertising or trade purposes." Others have merely said that privacy is invaded when the name or picture of a person is used in a way which offends the sensibilities of an ordinary person. We shall see later how the courts have refined and shaped these broad concepts to accommodate the needs of both public and individual.

If a photographer could get a release from every person of age who turns up in his pictures (and from the parents of every person not of age), he would have no problems with right-of-privacy suits. Getting a release, however, is not always easy and is a chore most people prefer to avoid. That is why it is absolutely essential to know when a release is necessary, and this requires some additional knowledge about the right of privacy.

History

Although the earliest intimations of this legal right can be traced back to ancient Jewish law, the concept of an enforceable right of privacy as we know it today dates from 1890. In that year, in an article in the *Harvard Law Review*,[2] Louis Brandeis (later Justice Brandeis) and Samuel D. Warren argued for recognition by the courts of the right of people to be secure in their private lives from interference by the press and undeserved publicity.

Almost simultaneously the courts were hearing cases in which an effort was made to invoke a right of privacy, and in some instances the complaining parties were successful.[3] But in 1902, in the now famous case of *Roberson v. Rochester Folding Box Co.*,[4] the right of privacy suffered a severe blow at the hands of the highest court in the State of New York. The case involved the appearance of posters and magazine advertisements for "Franklin Mills Flour" which were adorned with the photograph of a comely lass named Roberson. The purpose was to show that both Miss Roberson and the flour were of excellent quality and to entice the reader to at least try the product. Miss Roberson objected to the undesired publicity and sued for damages.

The court, however, did not come to the aid of the aggrieved Miss Roberson. Instead, it denied the existence of the right of privacy and held that no legal right had been violated. This decision resulted in a storm of criticism by the press, as well as general popular disapproval, and at the very next session of the New York State Legislature there was enacted into law a right of privacy.

The New York statute (reprinted at the end of this chapter) became the model for similar statutes in several other states, but the development of the right of privacy in this country has largely been by rule of court rather than by statute. At the present time the right of privacy has been held by the courts to exist in Alabama, Arizona, Arkansas, California, Colorado, Connecticut, Delaware, District of Columbia, Florida, Georgia, Idaho, Illinois, Indiana, Iowa, Kansas, Kentucky, Louisiana, Michigan, Missouri, Montana, New Jersey, North Carolina, Ohio, Oregon, Pennsylvania, South Carolina, South Dakota and West Virginia.

Still other states have followed the lead of New York in enacting statutes protecting the right of privacy. Such legislation has been enacted in Utah,[5] Virginia,[6] Wisconsin,[7] Oklahoma and Nebraska, although the prohibition of the Wisconsin statute merely applied to the publication (except as may be necessary in the institution or prosecution of a criminal proceeding) of the name of a woman who may have been raped or subjected to criminal assault. The Utah and Virginia statutes essentially follow the New York statute.

Despite the growth of the right of privacy during the last sixty years, it must be remembered that the doctrine is still very much in its infancy. The outlines of its nature and extent as sketched in judicial decisions are still rough and difficult to define. In many states even the existence of the right of privacy is still an undetermined question. For this reason the writer in this area of law hesitates to make broad, sweeping pronouncements concerning the status of the law of privacy.

We have already pointed out that in New York, by statute, a person's name or likeness may not be used for "advertising or trade" purposes without written consent. In states not having a statute similar to New York's, the courts inquire whether a particular use is offensive to the sensibilities of an ordinary person. The language used in the cases may be different, but with few exceptions the courts in the states where the right of privacy is recognized have arrived at similar results on similar sets of facts. In broad terms, the courts have applied the right of privacy to prevent unwarranted exploitation of one's personality without his consent.[8]

The Lahiri Case

In 1937 a right of privacy action was brought in the courts of New York by a professional Hindu musician as the result of the publication of a story in a New York newspaper concerning the "rope trick" performed by plaintiff.[9] The plaintiff's picture had been used to illustrate the story and he claimed an invasion of his privacy which violated the New York statute. Justice Shientag, in deciding that Lahiri's privacy had not been invaded, formulated four rules concerning the use of photographs to illustrate articles which have been applied by the courts of New York ever since and which are also cited by courts in other jurisdictions. The rules were summarized by Judge Hofstadter of the New York Supreme Court this way:

(1) Recovery under the statute may be had, if the photograph is published in or as part of an advertisement, or for advertising purposes;

(2) Recovery may be had, if the photograph is used in connection with a work of fiction;

(3) No recovery may be had if the photograph is published in connection with an article of current news or immediate public interest; and

(4) No recovery may be had, as a general rule, if the article is educational or informative in character.[10]

As to the last two categories, however, the courts have said that there may be an invasion of privacy "if the photograph used has so tenuous a connection with the news item or educational article that it can be said to have no legitimate relation to it and be used for the purpose of promoting the sale of the publication";[11] or, as the courts have said, if the use is such that it would be "repugnant to one's sense of decency," or would "outrage common ordinary decency."[12] Now let us see how the courts have applied the rules.

Advertising

The courts have usually had little difficulty in deciding what constitutes a use for "advertising purposes." Clearly, the display of a photograph in connection with the endorsement of a product is such a use. For example, where a woman paid a photographer to make a portrait of her, and the photographer, without the subject's consent, sold a copy of the portrait to a publisher who used it to promote the sale of a book on hair culture, a New York court said that the picture had been used for advertising purposes.[13] Thus, the determination by the photographer as to whether a picture is being used for advertising purposes is, in most cases, not a difficult task.

An interesting question arises, however, when a picture originally exempt from restrictions against invasion of privacy because it was a legitimate news picture used as such is republished for advertising purposes. A good illustration of the special rule here is the recent case of *Booth v. Curtis Publishing Co.*[14] *Holiday* magazine published a picture of actress Shirley Booth in a legitimate news article to which the picture was clearly relevant. Miss Booth did not complain about this original use, but when the picture was republished in advertisements for *Holiday* which appeared in the *New Yorker* and *Advertising Age,* she sued *Holiday's* publisher, claiming that her picture and name had been used for advertising and/or purposes of trade without her consent. The court, however, agreed with the defendant's argument that using news pictures to *advertise the publication in which they first appeared* is merely "incidental" to the privilege of using news pictures for legitimate news purposes, and comes within the same exemption.

In pointing out the difference between use of a news picture in "incidental" advertising of the news medium, and its use in "collateral" advertising, advertising of a product which has no direct connection with the magazine or newspaper in which the picture first appeared, the court in the *Booth* case discussed the case of *Flores v. Mosler Safe Co.,*[15] which had come up in New York a few years earlier. The court said this was a good example of "collateral" use of a news picture which constituted an invasion of privacy for which a plaintiff could recover. In this case, the Mosler Safe Company distributed a circular on which it reproduced, as a dramatic illustration of the danger to unprotected business records in case of fire, a striking picture of a burning building, together with the captions and news story which had accompanied the picture when it was originally published in a newspaper. The story made several references to the plaintiff. The court in that case held that although the material reproduced, both picture and story, was originally legitimate news material, it did not come within the "news" exemption to uses for advertising because the circular advertised safes rather than the newspaper which had published the story. The same rule would apply to similar use of a picture of a person (rather than a building) without the necessity of the additional use of the person's name.

Gautier v. Pro Football, Inc.[16] is an illustration of a case in which the New York Court of Appeals was asked to determine the application of the term "advertising purposes" to an unusual situation, and in which, as in the *Holiday* magazine case, it decided that there had been no violation of the Civil Rights Law.

In this case the plaintiff, a well-known trainer of animals, performed before an audience of 35,000 persons between the halves of a professional football game. He had not given his consent to the telecast of his performance, but the entire football game, including his performance, was in fact televised. In the course of the telecast, paid commercial announcements for Chesterfield cigarettes were made. There was one such commercial just before plaintiff's performance, and another just after his performance. Plaintiff urged that on the foregoing facts, his name and picture had been used for advertising purposes in violation of Sections 50 and 51 of the Civil Rights Law. The Court of Appeals affirmed the Appellate Division's decision that there had been no use of plaintiff's name or picture for advertising purposes. The court pointed out that although the telecast was paid for by Chesterfield, the entire program was not thereby a solicitation for patronage. The court said that "unless plaintiff's name or picture were in some way connected with the 'commercial,' the mere fact of sponsorship of the telecast would not . . . suffice to violate the statute in this respect."

In line with the *Booth v. Curtis Publishing Co.* case above, permitting the use of news pictures to advertise the publication in which they first appeared and calling such use "incidental" to the privilege of publishing news pictures for legitimate news purposes, another interesting case was decided in March, 1969, when an advertising use was held permissible by a publisher without the consent of the person involved. In *Rand v. Hearst Corp.,*[16a] the Appellate Division of the New York Supreme Court was called upon to decide at what point a public figure (in this case a well-known author) might complain when her style of writing was compared with that of another author and this comparison appeared on the cover of the other author's book. The court, in deciding that not every advertising use is prohibited, said:

> The law—narrowly written—attempts to do so by proscribing the use of the person's name or picture for the purposes of trade or advertising. However, it has already been clearly established that not in every instance where a person's picture or name is used in connection with advertising will a violation of the statute be found. (See *Booth v. Curtis Publishing Co.,* supra.) The *Booth* case presented a situation where a person's photograph was used for advertising purposes and yet it was held that plaintiff had no cause of action.
>
> [6] Thus, in construing the law, the courts have looked to its underlying purpose—the need it was intended to fill—and rather than adhering to its exact letter have interpreted the spirit in which it was written. The words "advertising purposes" and for the "purposes of trade" were used as the means to carry out the law's fundamental purpose—the pro-

tection of an individual's right of privacy. They must be construed narrowly and not used to curtail the right of free speech, or free press, or to shut off the publication of matters newsworthy or of public interest, or to prevent comment on matters in which the public has an interest or the right to be informed. Its underlying purpose being to protect privacy, in the case of a public figure—who by the very nature of being a public figure has no complete privacy—no liability exists when his or her name or picture is used without consent, or when the article complained of is of public interest, unless, of course, the publication is knowingly false (*Hemingway v. Random House, Inc.*, 23 N.Y. 2d 341, 296 N.Y.S. 2d 771, 244 N.E. 2d 250) or may be considered a blatant selfish, commercial exploitation of the individual's personality. (*Gautier v. Pro-Football*, supra.) As stated by the Court of Appeals in *Spahn*, and quoted with approval by the United States Supreme Court in *Time, Inc. v. Hill*, 385 U.S. 374, 382, 87 S.Ct. 534, 17 L.Ed. 2d 456, "ever mindful that the written word or picture is involved, courts have engrafted exceptions and restrictions on to the statute to avoid any conflict with the free dissemination of thoughts, ideas, newsworthy events, and matters of public interest." . . .

It is quite apparent, therefore, that books and publications have a special position in the law. My distinguished colleague in dissenting puts it very aptly when he states that "[concededly book publishing, though a business, stands on a somewhat different plane than many other businesses in that freedom of the press is often involved]." Therefore, in considering books and publications, courts must take a broad view of what may or may not be written and what may or may not be said about books and their authors.

Under the *Rand* case, which was unanimously affirmed by the Court of Appeals of New York, we have another exception to the prohibition against the use of one's name or picture for advertising purposes without consent where book publishing is involved, under the principle that the right to discuss the work of a public figure in the literary world, to comment on it, or to criticize and compare it is within the public domain. We therefore find the courts "engrafting" exceptions and restrictions upon the right of privacy statute to avoid conflict with the free dissemination of thoughts, ideas, newsworthy events and matters of public interest.

In still another case, which clearly appeared to involve an advertising use of a picture without permission, the court interpreted the right of privacy statute so as to relieve the publisher of a newspaper of liability. The case is of interest not only to publishers but to advertisers, advertising agencies, and photographers as well. The magazine supplement of the New York *Herald Tribune* published two pictures of a girl model at the beach wearing what was called a "Poor-Boy Swim Suit." Some young boys were playing or standing in the vicinity of the model when she was photographed. The model was posed. Although the boys just happened to be nearby, they were clearly identifiable in the pictures.

The beach scene pictures were published with a note, including captions, purporting to be a fashion item, which indicated that the "Poor-Boy Swim Suit" was directly descended from a "big fad fashion" of the previous winter, the "Poor-Boy Sweater," which was launched by the French magazine *Elle*. The note ended with a statement that "the suit is by Elon, $20. Lord & Taylor."

Action was brought on behalf of several of the boys, who were less than ten years of age, under the right of privacy statute on the ground that their pictures were used for advertising without permission. The newspaper's motion to dismiss the complaint in advance of the trial was denied, and the newspaper appealed. The Appellate Division of the New York Supreme Court, in a 3 to 2 decision, reversed the lower court and dismissed the complaint (*Pagan v. New York Herald Tribune*),[16b] holding that the use of the boys' pictures was not for advertising (although the accompanying fashion note referred to price and source where the item could be purchased) since they appeared only incidentally in the pictures. Consequently their use, in the light of the accompanying text, could be considered an item of legitimate public interest. The court said:

> Where a picture of an individual is published in a newspaper or magazine in connection with the presentation, without false or misleading material, of a matter of legitimate public interest to readers, and the picture bears a reasonable relationship to the presentation, the use of the picture in the publication is not actionable as a use for the purpose of advertising or trade within the prohibition of the statute unless the presentation is in effect an advertisement in disguise. . . .
>
> The decision in *La Forge v. Fairchild Publications,* supra, is sufficiently in point to be controlling. There, the defendant had published in its newspaper a two-page pictorial story entitled "Fashion Follows a Pattern." As noted in the memorandum of this court, the "spread" consisted of a dozen or more individual photographs taken at a racetrack of boys, young men and mature males each garbed in a sport jacket of a particular material. None of the individuals, including plaintiff, was identified by name or otherwise. The written matter accompanying the pictures stated, among other things, that the specified material of the jackets was a "runaway fashion at the races and associated events." This court concluded that the publication was not "for advertising purposes or for the purposes of trade" within the meaning of section 51 of the Civil Rights Law, citing *Dallesandro v. Henry Holt & Co.*, supra.

As mentioned above, this was a 3 to 2 decision. The dissenting judges felt that the case should not have been dismissed in advance of trial, because in their opinion there was an issue as to whether the picture and printed matter were "an advertisement in disguise."

In a recent case (*Porter v. New West Magazine*), the New York Supreme Court refused to grant a temporary injunction in advance of the trial to a professional model whose picture had been taken by a professional photographer for "test" purposes and sold by him to *New West Magazine Company*. A coupon was inserted with the photograph in an advertising brochure together with coupons for 20 other products for distribution to persons living in California, Arizona and Nevada. Defendants pleaded that they would make no further use of the picture, and since they no longer had any control of the previous use (with the coupons) they could not stop a scheduled mailing by R. H. Donnelly & Co. The court refused to grant the temporary injunction to the model since she had failed to show that she would suffer irreparable harm if the injunction were not granted. The court held that if the model could prove her case, she had other adequate legal remedies (which would include money damages). The decision said:

> As a professional model, the plaintiff seeks neither privacy nor anonymity. If she establishes a right to recover, it does not appear that her legal remedies will be inadequate.***

Articles of Fiction

Nor is the use of photographs to illustrate articles of fiction too difficult an area. Some years ago a story appeared in a national magazine about a gunner on a Flying Fortress who was shot down during World War II. He had left a strange will, in which he bequeathed "one perfect rose" a week to a young lady who was a casual acquaintance. The magazine printed the picture of the young lady, as well as her name, and she sued for invasion of privacy. The court found that the story was not basically true, that the author had drawn somewhat upon a vivid imagination, and allowed recovery.[17]

In the following sections we shall see other examples of articles of public interest that by reason of inaccuracy, falsehood or distortion turn out to be fictional and consequently a use for purposes of profit or trade. We shall also see how the special rules affecting publishers of newspapers and magazines are applied in this area.

Purposes of Trade

In dealing particularly with classifications 3 and 4 of the Lahiri case (pictures used to illustrate items of news, immediate public interest, or of an educational or informative nature) the courts have found it necessary to explain that one cannot classify the use of a picture in a publication as being for "trade purposes" merely because a publisher seeks to make a profit from his magazine or newspaper.

In one sense every picture published in a newspaper or magazine is for the purpose of increasing circulation and increasing profits. In a photographic magazine, for example, the objective of the material is to teach and exhibit photographic excellence, and the pictures are selected for that reason even though the publisher profits by virtue of showing better pictures.[18]

In determining what is news or a matter of immediate public interest, the courts have assiduously avoided interpretations which could lead to encroachments upon freedom of the press. The courts have held, for example, that a scene in a newsreel of a group of women in a gymnasium attempting to reduce by means of various apparatus was a matter of public interest and not an invasion of privacy,[19] and ruled similarly where a passerby happened to get caught in a film of a crowd at an event of current interest.[20]

In this connection, it is interesting to note a decision of a federal court in a case brought against Dell Publishing Co. as a result of the publication in *Front Page Detective* of a picture which originally appeared in Pittsburgh newspapers back in 1953.[21]

The plaintiffs in the case were the widow and children of a man who was kicked to death by hoodlums. In the January, 1954, issue of *Front Page Detective,* under the title of "Heartbreak House," there was a short account of the homicide and a picture. The suit was brought on a right of privacy theory and plaintiffs moved for summary judgment. The motion was denied by the U.S. District Court, and the Circuit Court affirmed. In arriving at its decision, the court said:

> But in this situation, the interest of the public in free dissemination of the truth and unimpeded access to news is so broad, so difficult to define and so dangerous to circumscribe that courts have been reluctant to make such factually accurate public disclosures tortious, except where the lack of any meritorious public interest in the disclosures is very clear and its offensiveness to ordinary sensibilities is equally clear.
>
> We concluded that the pictorially illustrated story of which plaintiffs complain is within the privilege which protects normal news items against claims of tortious invasion of privacy.

In a landmark case decided by the United States Supreme Court in January, 1967,[21a] the publishers of *Life* magazine were sued for falsely reporting that a new play portrayed an experience suffered by the Hill family. The article was entitled "True Crime Inspires Tense Play," with the subtitle "The ordeal of a family trapped by convicts gives Broadway a new thriller 'The Desperate Hours.' " The article then went on to show how a family rose to heroism in a crisis. *Life* magazine photographed the play, published some of the scenes, transported some of the actors to the house where the Hills had been held hostage, and re-enacted scenes from the play, which it also published. The pictures included shots of Hill's son being roughed up by one of the convicts, captioned "brutish convict," a picture of Hill's daughter biting the hand of a convict to make him drop a gun, captioned "daring daughter," and a picture of the father throwing his gun through the door after a "brave try" to save his family was foiled.

The facts were that the Hill family had been the subject of a front page story three years before as a result of having been held hostage for 19 hours by three escaped convicts in their suburban home in Whitemarsh, Pa. The family was released unharmed, and in an interview held with newsmen after the convicts departed, Mr. Hill stressed that the convicts had not molested them and had not been violent. The convicts were subsequently apprehended in an encounter with the police in which two of the convicts were killed. Thereafter, the Hill family moved to Connecticut and discouraged all efforts to keep them in the public spotlight through magazine stories or appearances on television.

The novel *The Desperate Hours* was published the year following the incident, but unlike the actual experience, the family in the story suffered violence at the hands of the convicts; the father and son were beaten, and the daughter subjected to verbal sexual insult. The book was then made into a play, *The Desperate Hours,* and *Life's* article concerning the play resulted in the lawsuit brought by the Hill family.

Life's defense was that the article was the subject of legitimate news interest and a subject of general interest and concern to the public at the time of publication and that it was published in good faith without any malice.

After the Hills won in the lower courts, *Life* appealed. The Appellate Courts affirmed the decision, and *Life* appealed to the United States Supreme Court, which heard argument on the case twice. Richard M. Nixon represented the Hills before the United States Supreme Court. However, notwithstanding the eminent counsel who later became our President, the Supreme Court set aside the judgment in favor of the Hills. The court said that the constitutional protection of free expression precludes the right of privacy action to redress false reports of newsworthy matters in the absence of proof that the publisher knew of such falsity or acted in reckless disregard of the truth. The court further ruled that erroneous statements about a matter of public interest, such as the opening of a new play linked to an actual incident, are inevitable and, if innocent or merely negligent, must be protected if freedoms of expression are to have the "breathing space" that they "need to survive." The court warned, however, that there is no constitutional protection of calculated falsehoods. Since the jury that had awarded $30,000 to the Hills after a second trial had not been properly instructed that such a verdict could only be predicated on a finding of knowing or reckless falsity in the publication of the article, the judgment was set aside and the case remanded for further proceedings.

The Supreme Court emphasized in the *Hill* case that a publication is not required to assume the impossible burden of verifying to a degree of certainty facts set forth in a news article associated with a person's picture or name and that liability will be imposed only where there is a calculated falsehood or reckless disregard for the truth:

We create a grave risk of serious impairment of the indispensable service of a free press in a free society if we saddle the press with the impossible burden of verifying to a certainty the facts associated in news articles with a person's name, picture or portrait, particularly as related to non-defamatory matter. Even negligence would be a most elusive standard, especially when the content of the speech itself affords no warning of prospective harm to another through falsity. A negligence test would place on the press the intolerable burden of guessing how a jury might assess the reasonableness of steps taken by it to verify the accuracy of every reference to a name, picture or portrait.

In this context, sanctions against either innocent or negligent mis-statement would present a grave hazard of discouraging the press from exercising the constitutional guarantees. Those guarantees are not for the benefit of the press so much as for the benefit of all of us. A broadly defined freedom of the press assures the maintenance of our political system and an open society. Fear of large verdicts in damage suits for innocent or merely negligent misstatement, even fear of the expense in-volved in their defense, must inevitably cause publishers to "steer . . . wider of the unlawful zone," *New York Times Co. v. Sullivan,* 376 U.S., at 279; see also *Speiser v. Randall,* 357 U.S. 513, 526; *Smith v. California,* 361 U.S. 147, 153-154; and thus "create the danger that the legitimate utter-ance will be penalized." *Speiser v. Randall,* supra, at 526.

But the constitutional guarantees can tolerate sanctions against *cal-culated* falsehood without significant impairment of their essential func-tion. We held in *New York Times* that calculated falsehood enjoyed no immunity in the case of alleged defamation of a public official concerning his official conduct. Similarly, calculated falsehood should enjoy no im-munity in the situation here presented us.

The *Hill* case is discussed under the heading of *purposes of trade* since one of the points raised by the Hills was that fictionalizing certain aspects of the story was done for purposes of trade; however, this case also fits under the headings of *fiction* and *public figures,* since the Hills did achieve wide publicity as a result of the experience where they were held as hostages.

In a more recent case (*Wojtowicz v. Delacorte Press,* N.Y. Supreme Ct.)[21b] along the line of the Hill case, the plaintiff brought suit against a book publisher and movie studio in her own behalf as well as in behalf of her in-fant children. The plaintiff was the wife of a would-be bank robber whose exploits, whether real or fictionalized, were portrayed in a film and thereafter in a book entitled *Dog Day Afternoon.* She alleged that her name, portrait and picture and those of her children, were used without her consent for pur-poses of "trade or advertising" in order to induce members of the public to purchase books and theatre tickets. She also sued for damages to the children by reason of defamation of their mother (the adult plaintiff). "Dog Day Afternoon" was one of the top motion pictures of 1975 commercially and artistically as it earned substantial profits for its director and star. The film was based upon an actual aborted bank robbery with the proceeds of the crime intended for a sex-change operation. The picture was so successful that it was turned into a book. The case came to light when defendants made a motion in court to dismiss the major causes of action (the case has not yet come to trial). The court refused the dismissal motion, calling it premature. The court said that there were factual questions and disputes which require a resolution by trial. The judge said that there is an absence of clear precedents governing rights of privacy and standing to sue based on fictionalized episodes. For example, it appears "dubious" that the plaintiff's cause of action could be sustained under the New York Civil Rights Law unless it be established that the fictionalized name used and the portraying actress are both similar to plaintiff's name and appearance. He also said that there is an expanding recognition of right of privacy actions under recent U. S. Supreme Court decisions, including *Griswold v. Connecticut,* 381 U.S. 479, and *Roe v. Wade,* 410 U.S. 113, and such actions exist irrespective of the limiting rights under the provisions of the Civil Rights Law. Offsetting plaintiff's rights, the judge said, were other problems such as the rights of defendants under the First Amendment to the Federal Constitution and the extent to which "privacy," the right to be let alone, will be protected.

Of particular interest and importance was the court's definition of a "picture" within the meaning of the New York Civil Rights Law:

> A picture within the meaning of the statute is not necessarily a photograph of the living person, but includes any representation of such person. The picture represented by the defendant to be a true picture of the plaintiff and exhibited to the public as such, was intended to be, and it was, a representation of plaintiff. The defendant is in no position to say that the picture does not represent the plaintiff or that it was an actual picture of a person made up to look like and impersonate the plaintiff (*Birns v. Vitagraph Co.,* 210 N.Y. 51, 57). Birns, however, has been limited in subsequent decisional holding to its facts, that is an instance where not only the look-alike actor appears, but where the plaintiff's name is also used (*Toscani v. Hersey,* 271 App. Div. 445, 448). Such being the state of the law, it is dubious that the plaintiff has a cause of action under sections 50 and 51 of the Civil Rights Law (of New York) unless it be established that the fictionalized name used and the portraying actress are both so similar to plaintiff's name and appearance that the doctrine of Birns, supra, may be invoked. However, even if the action is not sustainable under the cited Civil Rights Law sections, if, from all of the papers, another cause of action is made out, no dismissal should result.

The court therefore left open to plaintiffs the opportunity to offer any proof of invasion of their right to privacy, saying:

> It is not necessary to recount here the revolting description of plaintiffs alleged to exist in both the film and book. If, as plaintiffs contend and appears likely, these plaintiffs, who have done nothing to make public figures of themselves (cf. *Spahn v. Julian Messner, Inc.,* 21 N.Y. 2d 124)

have, for the purposes of defendants' profits, had their lives invaded, de-
graded and fictionalized, a cause of action for invasion of privacy may
exist.

Before leaving the heading *purposes of trade,* we might add a word
about the display of pictures by a studio photographer. Under the New York
right of privacy statute, the photographer may display pictures about his
studio as samples of his work. This is not considered a use for trade purposes. If the subject objects, however, the photographer must remove the
picture.

Public Figures

It has also been generally settled that public figures have little right of
privacy. A statesman, actor, musician, or inventor who asks for and desires
public recognition in a large sense surrenders his right of privacy to the public. When one obtains a photograph of such a person, and there is no breach
of contract or confidence in the method in which it was obtained, he has the
right to reproduce it, for informative purposes, whether in a newspaper, magazine or book.

One of the most interesting cases in this area involved the publication
by the *New Yorker* magazine of a profile or biographical sketch in 1937. The
plaintiff had been a child prodigy and had graduated from Harvard at the age
of 16, at which time he received considerable publicity. The profile showed
that the plaintiff had since become an eccentric recluse, and exposed in merci-
less fashion the failure of the plaintiff to live up to his early promise. Plaintiff sued for invasion of privacy and the court ruled for the defendant on the
ground that plaintiff had been a public figure when a child, and that in 1937
there was still legitimate public interest in his career.[22]

The right of a public figure to privacy is clearly quite limited. One
court said: "Persons who accept high positions ought not to be so tender
about the mention of their names, they must bear 'the white light that beats
upon a throne.' "[23]

On the other hand, the privilege of using the picture of a famous person as a subject of news or current interest or for informative purposes does
not extend to the commercialization of his personality through forms of treatment distinct from dissemination of news or information.

In one case, a company had contracted with a number of baseball
players to use, exclusively, the players' photographs in connection with the
sale of the company's chewing gum. The defendant, a competing chewing
gum company, used photographs of the same players in connection with the
sale of its own chewing gum without plaintiff's consent. The first company
brought an action against its competitor in the Federal courts and the court,
in supporting the position of the plaintiff, pointed out that, in addition to and

independent of the right of privacy, a man has a right in the publicity value of his photograph; that this right was particularly important to prominent persons and that far from having their feelings bruised through public exposure of their likenesses, they would feel sorely deprived if they no longer received money for authorizing advertisements and other commercial display of their likenesses. The court referred to this right as a "right of publicity." In effect, the court was pointing out that a baseball player's name and picture were valuable items and that he had a right to expect income from the commercial exploitation of his personality.[24]

In another case involving a famous baseball player (*Spahn v. Messner*),[24a] Warren Spahn sought an injunction and damages against the unauthorized publication of what purported to be a biography of his life. The trial judge had found that "the record unequivocally establishes that the book publicizes areas of Warren Spahn's personal and private life albeit inaccurate and distorted and consists of a host, a preponderant percentage of factual errors, distortions and fanciful passages." The Court of Appeals of New York held that in these circumstances the publication was prohibited under the right of privacy statute and was not within the exceptions and restrictions between Spahn's professional career, as to which no right of privacy exists, and the exploitation of his personality for commercial benefit, as to which his right of privacy clearly exists. The court said:

> But, it is erroneous to confuse privacy with "personality" or to assume that privacy, though lost for a certain time or in a certain context goes forever unprotected. . . . Thus it may be appropriate to say that the plaintiff here, Warren Spahn, is a public personality and that, insofar as his professional career is involved, he is substantially without a right to privacy. That is not to say, however, that his "personality" may be fictionalized and that, as fictionalized, it may be exploited for the defendants' commercial benefit through the medium of an unauthorized biography.

This portion of the opinion was quoted with approval by the United States Supreme Court in the *Hill* case discussed above.

The *Spahn* case, originally decided in October, 1966, was reargued in the Court of Appeals on remand by the United States Supreme Court, and on reconsideration the court adhered to its original decision in favor of Warren Spahn. The court's decision on the reconsideration, which came down in December, 1967, stated as follows:

> The remand of this appeal by the Supreme Court gives us an opportunity to construe the statute so as to preserve its constitutionality . . . and to review the appeal in light of the standards set forth in *New York Times Co. v. Sullivan* (supra) and *Time, Inc. v. Hill.* . . .
> [1] We hold in conformity with our policy of construing sections 50 and 51 so as to fully protect free speech, that, before recovery by a public figure may be had for an unauthorized presentation of his life, it

must be shown in addition to the other requirements of the statute, that the presentation is infected with material and substantial falsification and that the work was published with knowledge of such falsification or with a reckless disregard for the truth.

[2] An examination of the undisputed findings of fact below as well as the defendants' own admission that "[i]n writing this biography, the author used the literary techniques of invented dialogue, imaginary incidents, and attributed thoughts and feelings" (brief for appellants, p. 10) clearly indicates that the test of *New York Times Co. v. Sullivan* (supra) and *Time, Inc. v. Hill* (supra) has been met here.

In another case decided by New York State's highest court, in December, 1968 (*Estate of Ernest Hemingway v. Random House Inc.*),[24b] the estate of this famous writer and his widow sought damages and an injunction against the author and publisher of a biography of Ernest Hemingway. Two of the grounds upon which the suit was based were that the author had wrongfully used material imparted in confidence and that the biography invaded the widow's right to privacy. The case was dismissed, and the dismissal upheld by the Appellate courts.

As to the right of privacy phase of the case, the Court of Appeals, in line with the *Spahn* and *Hill* cases ruled that a public figure—Mrs. Hemingway was held to be a public figure—may not bar the publication of an item of public interest in the absence of proof that the published matter was false and was published with knowledge of such falsity or in reckless disregard of the truth. The court said:

[13, 14] The fourth count—in which only Hemingway's widow asserts a cause of action—is grounded on the claim that the Hotchner book intrudes upon her privacy in violation of section 51 of the Civil Rights Law. The decisions in *Time, Inc. v. Hill*, 385 U.S. 374, 87 S.Ct. 534, supra, and *Spahn v. Julian Messner, Inc.*, 21 N.Y. 2d 124, 286 N.Y.S. 2d 832, 233 N.E. 2d 840, dispose of the point and confirm the correctness of the dismissal of this cause of action. Both of those cases establish that, in the light of constitutional guarantees of free speech, section 51 may not be applied to afford recovery to a public figure or in matters of public interest—to quote from *Hill*, 385 U.S. at p. 388, 87 S.Ct. at p. 542—"in the absence of proof that the defendant published the [item] with knowledge of its falsity or in reckless disregard of the truth." (See, also, *Spahn*, 21 N.Y. 2d. . . .) That Mrs. Hemingway is a public figure and newsworthy, within the meaning of these cases, may not be disputed. Not only is she the widow of a literary figure of world renown, a Nobel Laureate, but she herself has encouraged public attention to her status by writing articles for the popular magazines dealing with her husband and with events in their lives together. As the court aptly noted in *Goelet v. Confidential, Inc.*, 5 A.D. 2d 226, 228, 171 N.Y.S. 2d 223, 225, "[o]nce a person has sought publicity he cannot at his whim withdraw the events of his life from public scrutiny."

[15] With respect to the required proof of falsification, under the doctrine of the *Hill* and *Spahn* cases, we need but note that, despite a passing reference to the subject in an affidavit, no serious attempt was made to support such a claim. There was no allegation in the complaint of any misstatement knowingly or recklessly made, and in the proceedings below—as the court at Special Term (MURPHY, J.) observed—counsel for the plaintiff appears to have "conceded" that no issue was presented as to the existence of "misstatements, inaccuracies or untruths." Our study of the papers before us confirms this conclusion.

In still another case (*Rosemont Enterprises Inc. v. Random House Inc. and John Keats*),[24c] the New York Supreme Court decided that a biography of a public figure such as Howard Hughes falls within the constitutional protection for free speech and press and that no redress is available even for material and substantial falsification in the absence of proof that the book was published with knowledge of such falsity or in reckless disregard for the truth. The court further held that a public figure has no exclusive rights to his own life story and others need no consent or permission to write his biography. The court said:

[9, 10] The biography of Howard Hughes, published by defendants herein, irrespective of its literary merit or style . . . falls within those "reports of newsworthy people or events" which are constitutionally protected and which are outside the proscription of the New York "Rights of Privacy" statute. The allegation that the book was published for "purposes of trade" and profit does not as plaintiff seeks to imply, alter its protected status. The publication of a newspaper, magazine, or book which imparts truthful news or other factual information to the public does not fall within "the purposes of trade" contemplated by the New York statute, even though such publication is published and sold for a profit. (See *Time, Inc. v. Hill.* . . .)
[11-13] The remaining ground on which plaintiff seeks to justify this suit is the assignment to it of Hughes' "right of publicity." This is a right that recognizes the pecuniary value which attaches to the names and pictures of public figures, particularly athletes and entertainers, and the right of such people to this financial benefit. It is not, however, every public use of a prominent person's name that he has a right to exploit financially. It is the unauthorized use in connection with the sale of a commodity for *advertising* purposes which is recognized as an actionable wrong under New York law. The same requirement of commercial use which limits the New York right of privacy inheres in the "right of publicity." (*Chaplin v. National Broadcasting Co.*, D.C., 15 F.R.D. 134; cf. *Haelan Laboratories v. Topps Chewing Gum*, 202 F. 2d 866.) The publication of a biography is clearly outside the ambit of the "commercial use" contemplated by the "right of publicity" and such right can have no application to the publication of factual material which is constitutionally protected. Just as a public figure's "right of privacy" must yield to the public interest so too must the "right of publicity" bow where such

conflicts with the free dissemination of thoughts, ideas, newsworthy events, and matters of public interest.

[14] Because of such considerations, a public figure can have no exclusive rights to his own life story, and others need no consent or permission of the subject to write a biography of a celebrity. (See Hofstadter & Horowitz, *The Right of Privacy. . . .*)

In states which do not recognize the "right of publicity" as such,[25] the courts will often decide the same way on the same facts, speaking in terms of some limit to a public figure's waiver of his right of privacy. For example, in the case of *Bell v. Birmingham Broadcasting Co.*,[25a] the defendant broadcasting company caused an article to be published which included a photograph of announcer George Bell and the statement that Bell would announce all the University of Alabama football games for defendant that season. The fact was that although Bell and the broadcasting company had "opened negotiations" with respect to having Bell announce the games, they had not concluded a deal. Bell sued, charging that his name and picture had been used for purposes of trade without his consent. The court held the article was really in the nature of an advertisement and that this was an invasion of privacy. Although Bell, as a public figure, had relinquished part of his right of privacy, he was still entitled to be protected from unauthorized commercial exploitation.

In a rather unusual case the television comedian Pat Paulsen, who conducted a mock campaign for the Presidency in 1968, sued to enjoin defendant from marketing a poster embodying his picture (*Paulsen v. Personality Posters Inc.*, N.Y. Supreme Court).[25b] The poster was made up from an unpublished photograph belonging to Pat Paulsen which had been sent to defendant by his agent. The arrangement under which the picture was sent to defendant was sharply in dispute. Paulsen claimed that the picture was sent with an inquiry as to whether defendant would be interested in negotiating a license agreement with royalties for its use. The defendant, on the other hand, claimed that it was sent unsolicited with a request that it distribute the picture in poster form to aid a publicity campaign on behalf of Paulsen. The court denied Paulsen's application for a preliminary injunction, holding that the right of privacy statute was not intended to limit activities involving dissemination of news or information concerning matters of public interest and that such activities are privileged and do not fall within the scope of purposes of trade even though they are carried on for a profit. The unusual part of this case was that Paulsen claimed he was only kidding and his presidential activities were just a publicity stunt. Nevertheless, this was held to be a matter of public interest. The judge said:

It is apparently plaintiff's position that since "he is only kidding" and his presidential activities are really only a "publicity stunt" they fall outside the scope of constitutionally protected matters of public interest. Such premise is wholly untenable. When a well-known entertainer enters the presidential ring, tongue in cheek or otherwise, it is clearly newsworthy and of public interest. A poster which portrays plaintiff in that role, and reflects the spirit in which he approaches said role, is a form of public interest presentation to which protection must be extended. That the format may deviate from traditional patterns of political commentary, or that to some it may appear more entertaining than informing, would not alter its protected status. It is not for this or any court to pass value judgments predicated upon ephemeral subjective considerations which would serve to stifle free expression. "What is one man's amusement, teaches another's doctrine." (*Winters v. People of State of New York,* 333 U.S. 507, 510, 68 S.Ct. 665, 667, 92 L.Ed. 840.) Thus, whether the poster involved be considered as a significant satirical commentary upon the current presidential contest, or merely as a humorous presentation of a well-known entertainer's publicity gambit, or in any other light, be it social criticism or pure entertainment, it is sufficiently relevant to a matter of public interest to be a form of expression which is constitutionally protected and "deserving of substantial freedom."

Before leaving the subject of public figures, our readers should be aware of the recent United States Supreme Court decision in *Time Inc. v. Firestone* (discussed in Chapter VII on Libel by Photograph) in which the Court reviews the criteria for determining what turns a person into a public figure and comes up with the conclusion that things aren't always what they seem, and one who is cast into the public limelight by some private situation (which in the Firestone case was a divorce action) does not necessarily become a public figure).[26]

The Galella v Onassis Case

The *Galella v. Onassis* case[2a] (referred to in Chapter I in connection with the subject of where pictures may be taken) is a landmark case on right of privacy as well, and portends the recognition by the courts of a person's right to privacy as the right to be let alone and not be harassed by photographers to the point of emotional distress. A discussion of the facts will help the reader understand the impact of this decision.

Ronald Galella, a free-lance photographer specializing in photographs of well known persons brought suit against Jacqueline Onassis, the widow of the late President John F. Kennedy, and three U. S. Government secret service agents assigned the duty of protecting children of deceased presidents up to the age of 16 years.

The photographer sued for false arrest, malicious prosecution and interference with trade (the pursuit of his work as a professional photographer). The United States Government intervened in the action and the court not only dismissed the photographer's case but granted injunctive relief to Mrs. Onassis on her counter suit based on the photographer's harassment of her and her children.

The court in describing the photographer, said:

Galella fancies himself as a "paparazzo" (literally a kind of annoying insect, perhaps equivalent to the English "gadfly"). Paparazzi make themselves as visible to the public and obnoxious to their photographic subjects as possible to aid in the advertisement and wide sale of their works.

The court's opinion pointed out some examples of the photographer's conduct brought out at the trial. Galella took pictures of John Kennedy riding his bicycle in Central Park across the way from his home. He jumped out into the boy's path, causing the agents' concern for John's safety. The agents' reaction and interrogation of Galella led to Galella's arrest and his action against the agents; Galella on other occasions interrupted Caroline at tennis, and invaded the children's privacy in school. At one time he came uncomfortably close in a power boat to Mrs. Onassis while she was swimming. He often jumped and postured around while taking pictures of her party, notably at a theater opening, but also on numerous other occasions. He followed a practice of giving gratuities to apartment house, restaurant, and nightclub doormen as well as romancing a family servant to keep him advised of the movements of the family.

The court held that:

1. Secret service agents charged with protection of children of a deceased president were immune from liability for actions within the scope of their authority with respect to the arrest of the photographer who allegedly endangered one of the children.

2. The evidence supported the finding that the photographer was guilty of harassment, intentional infliction of emotional distress, assault and battery, invasion of privacy and commercial exploitation of the personality of the president's widow.

3. Privacy essential to individual dignity and personal liberty underlies the fundamental rights guaranteed in the Bill of Rights under the Constitution.

4. That aside from right of privacy, the injunction against the photographer was sustainable under New York State's proscription of harassment under the Penal Law of that state.

5. Legitimate countervailing social needs may warrant some intrusion despite an individual's reasonable expectation of privacy and freedom from harassment but the interference allowed may be no greater than that necessary to protect the overriding public interest.

6. Although the widow of a president was a public figure and therefore subject to news coverage, the photographer went far beyond reasonable bounds of news gathering by his constant surveillance and by his obtrusive and intruding presence.

7. The First Amendment guaranteeing a freedom of speech and press does not establish a wall of immunity which protects newsmen from all liability for their conduct while gathering news; that crimes

and torts committed in news gathering are not protected by the First Amendment. Furthermore, there is no threat to a free press in requiring newsmen to act within the law.

8. Testimony of the president's widow as to mental distress caused by the photographer's surveillance of her could properly be admitted into evidence on her claim against the photographer for harassment. Furthermore, the children's reaction to the photographer's antics was also admissible even though based on hearsay declarations.

It is interesting to note that this decision of the United States District Court for the Southern District (353 F. Suppl. 196) was appealed by the photographer to the United States Court of Appeals (Second Circuit) 487 Fed. 2nd 990. The decision was affirmed except that an injunction issued by the trial court which required the photographer to stay 100 yards from the home of Mrs. Onassis and 50 yards from her personally was modified to prohibit only an approach within 25 feet of her or the touching of her person as well as any blocking of her movement in public places and thoroughfares and any act foreseeably or reasonably calculated to place her life or safety in jeopardy and any conduct which could reasonably be foreseen to harass, alarm or frighten her. However, the court held that the photographer could not properly be enjoined from taking and selling pictures of Mrs. Onassis for news coverage. Of course, the photographer was also enjoined from interfering with the secret service agents' duties of protecting the children and would not be permitted to enter the children's schools or play areas, to engage in action calculated to or reasonably foreseen to place their safety or well-being in jeopardy; nor would the photographer be permitted to harass, alarm or frighten the children and would not be permitted to approach within 30 feet of them.

As is evident from the multi-faceted rulings in this case it is a decision of primary importance.

However, we consider the most important aspect of the case, the pronouncement that the New York courts may be ready to recognize a common law right to privacy and may be ready when again faced with the issue presented in the 1902 case of *Roberson v. Rochester Folding Box* (discussed at the outset of this chapter) to modify or overrule that decision.

The following footnote and discussion indicates the readiness of the courts to accept the recognition of a common law right to privacy:

Although the New York courts have not yet recognized a common law right of privacy, if we were required to reach the question, we would be inclined to agree with the court below that when again faced with the issue, the Court of Appeals may well modify or distinguish its 1902 holding in *Roberson v. Rochester Folding-Box Co.*, 171 N.Y. 538 64 N.E. 442 (1902), that "The so-called right of privacy has not as yet found an abiding place in our jurisprudence." There is substantive support today for the proposition that privacy is a "basic right" entitled to legal protection, *Time v. Hill*, 385 U.S. 374, 415, 87 S.Ct. 534, 17 L.Ed.

2d 456 (1967) (Fortas, J., dissenting), nor can the "power of a State to control and remedy such intrusion (even) for news gathering purposes . . . be denied." Id. at 404, 87 S.Ct. at 550 (Harlan, J., concurring and dissenting). Privacy essential to individual dignity and personal liberty underlies the fundamental rights guaranteed in the Bill of Rights. See *Katz v. United States*, 389 U.S. 347, 350 n. 5, 88 S.Ct. 507, 19 L.Ed. 2d 576 (1967); *Tehan v. U.S.* ex rel. Shott, 382 U.S. 406, 416, 86 S.Ct. 459, 15 L.Ed. 2d 453 (1966) (Fifth Amendment); *Stanley v. Georgia*, 394 U.S. 557, 564-566, 89 S.Ct. 1243, 22 L.Ed. 2d 542 (1969) (First and Fourteenth Amendments). See also *Time v. Hill*, supra, 385 U.S. at 412-415, 87 S.Ct. 534; Bloustein, Privacy as an Aspect of Human Dignity: An Answer to Dean Prosser, 39 N.Y.U. L.Rev. 962, 971 (1964); Fried, Privacy, 77 Yale L.J. 475, 482ff (1968). There is an emerging recognition of privacy as a distinct, constitutionally protected right. *Roe v. Ingraham*, 480, F. 2d 102 (2d Cir., 1973), (Friendly, J).

While the Constitution provides protection for specific manifestations of privacy ". . . the protection of a person's general right to privacy—his right to be let alone by other people is like the protection of his property and his very life left largely to the law of the individual states. . . ." Katz, supra, 389 U.S. at 350-351, 88 S.Ct. at 511, citing Warren & Brandeis, Right to Privacy, 4 Harv. L. Rev. 193 (1890).

The vast majority of states have now recognized and protect a right to privacy. Restatement of Torts 2d § 652(a), comment a (Tent. Draft No. 13, 1967) statutory protection has been afforded the right in New York through imposition of criminal sanctions for invasion of privacy through the use of mechanical devices for wiretap and eavesdropping and for tampering with certain private communications. New York Penal Code 250.00-250.35 (McKinney, 1967).

Although not recognizing a right to privacy as such except as defined by statute, the New York courts have softened this rule in many cases by recognizing and liberally applying freedom from emotional distress as a protectable interest. See *Long v. Beneficial Finance Co. of New York*, 39 A.D. 2d 11, 330 N.Y.S. 2d 664, 667-668 (1972); *Halio v. Lurie*, 15 A.D. 2d 62, 222 N.Y.S. 2d 759, 763-764 (1961); *Callarama v.. Associates Discount Corp. of Delaware*, 69 Misc. 2d 287, 329 N.Y.S. 2d 711 (1972); *Ruiz v. Bertolotti*, 37 Misc. 2d 1067, 236 N.Y.S. 2d 854 (1962), aff'd mem. 20 A.D. 2d 628, 245 N.Y.S. 2d 1003 (1963).

Informative and Educational Articles

The area of informative and educational articles (and the use of photographs to illustrate them) lies somewhere between current news and fiction. Here is how Justice Shientag described such articles in the Lahiri case:

They are not the responses to an event of peculiarly immediate interest, but, though based on fact, are used to satisfy an ever-present educational need. Such articles include, among others, travel stories, stories of distant places, tales of historic personages and events, the reproduction of items of past news and surveys of social conditions. These are articles educational and informative in character. As a general rule such cases are not within the purview of the statute.[27]

It is in this area that the courts appear to have the greatest difficulty striking a proper balance between the public interest in the dissemination of information and the preservation of an individual's privacy. One interesting case in New York, *Callas v. Whisper*,[28] involved the publication in a magazine of a photograph of plaintiff in a nightclub with a male companion. Plaintiff was merely a background figure in the photograph, which had been posed for the purpose of showing another person. The complaint alleged that plaintiff was an employee in the office of the publisher in a clerical capacity and that she had permitted defendants to take her picture upon the express understanding that they would not publish it. Plaintiff complained that the publication of her picture in a magazine which contained sensational and lurid articles gave the impression that she had been in a night club with a male companion and that she smoked and drank intoxicating beverages. The case was dismissed in advance of the trial, on the ground that it appeared from the plaintiff's own statement of her case in the court that the picture had not been used for advertising purposes or purposes of trade, and this decision was affirmed by the highest court in the State of New York.

In *Oma v. Hillman Periodicals, Inc., Pageant* magazine printed an article about the boxing profession. On the back cover appeared a photograph of plaintiff, identified by name, while the article made no mention of plaintiff whatsoever. The caption under the photograph referred the reader to the article inside. The court dismissed plaintiff's complaint based on violation of the Civil Rights Law, Sections 50 and 51, saying that this publication was not for the purposes of trade or advertising, but to illustrate an article of public interest. Explaining its conclusion further, the court[28a] noted that the illustration was relevant to the story, and it is immaterial that it was also used to sell the article.

The case of *Dallesandro v. Henry Holt & Co.*,[28b] decided in 1957 by the Appellate Division in New York, involved a complaint under the New York Privacy Law, by a dock worker whose photograph appeared on the cover of a book entitled *Waterfront Priest*. The plaintiff was not identified by name on the cover or in the text of the book. The court, affirming dismissal of the complaint, stated:

> The book here involved purports to be the true story of a priest's "one-man crusade against gangsterism and terror on the New York Waterfront," and the book jacket showing the priest in earnest conversation with a longshoreman is an attempted pictorialization of the theme.
>
> It is immaterial that its manner of use and placement was designed to sell the articles so that it might be paid for and read (*Oma v. Hillman Periodicals, Inc.,* supra, 281. App. Div. at page 244, 118 N.Y.S. 2d at

page 724). . . . The offending book jacket is annexed to the complaint, and since it appears therefrom that the use of the picture is not actionable under the civil rights law, the complaint was properly dismissed without leave to amend

Yet in another cover-photograph case decided in New York (*Murray v. N.Y. Magazine Co.*),[28c] the Appellate Division of the Supreme Court in a 3 to 2 decision refused to grant the motion of the defendant magazine to dismiss without a trial the complaint of a person who was photographed on a public street wearing an Irish hat while watching the St. Patrick's Day parade. The picture appeared on the March 17, 1969, cover of the defendant's magazine without the plaintiff's consent. The magazine featured several articles, including one entitled "The Last of the Irish Immigrants." The dissenting judges held that since the photograph appeared in an issue that was published on St. Patrick's Day, it bore a reasonable connection to a matter of legitimate public interest, even though the picture had been taken two years before, and they cited the *Dallesandro v. Holt* case in support of their dissent. However, the majority of the court held that plaintiff is entitled to a trial on these facts. (It is difficult to reconcile this case with the decision in the *Dallesandro* case.)

We trust the cases described will at least show the photographer the broad outlines of the factors considered by the courts in this area.

The Decency Test

In most cases which have arisen outside of New York and the other statutory states listed previously, the courts have sought to determine whether a photograph would be offensive to the sensitivities of an ordinary person. In an action brought in the Federal courts some years ago,[29] Eleanor Sue Leverton, a minor, sued the Curtis Publishing Company for wrongful invasion of her right of privacy by publication of her photograph as she lay in the street immediately after being struck by an automobile. The photograph had originally appeared in a daily newspaper the day after the accident. Twenty months later, it was used by the Curtis Publishing Company as an illustration for an article on traffic accidents with emphasis on pedestrian carelessness under the title, "They Asked to Be Killed." The court's decision for the plaintiff rested on two grounds:

(1) Even though the picture might not have lost its newsworthiness over a period of 20 months, the use of it to illustrate an article unrelated to the particular accident was not newsworthy and could, therefore, not be published under this exception to the rules governing invasion of the right of privacy.

(2) The question whether the publication of the photograph was offensive to ordinary sensibilities should be submitted to the jury.

In still another case, brought in California,[30] the publication of the photograph of a husband and wife in an affectionate position in a national magazine as part of an article on "Love" was held to be an invasion of privacy. Plaintiffs had been photographed while embracing and underneath the photograph appeared the caption, "Publicized as glamorous, desirable, 'Love at first sight' is a bad risk." Among other things, the court said that it was not unreasonable to believe the picture would be humiliating and disturbing to plaintiff's sensibilities, and that it could find no pertinency to the picture that would justify its use without consent. Note that the photograph in this case might, under some circumstances, be considered libelous because of its implications.

Distinction Between Defamation and Right of Privacy

It is important for photographers to recognize the distinction between libel and the right of privacy. The two are often confused, but there are several differences which can be readily observed. First, libel is an injury to reputation—that is, injury in the eyes of others—while invasion of privacy involves an injury to one's own feelings—the right to be let alone.[31] In the case of the latter, it does not matter whether the publication has any effect on reputation. Second, truth is generally a defense in libel actions. Truth is no defense to an action for invasion of the right of privacy.

The United States Supreme Court in *New York Times Co. v. Sullivan*,[31a] formulated a guideline limiting the permissible scope of defamation actions by announcing "a federal rule that prohibits a *public official* from recovering damages for a defamatory falsehood relating to his official conduct unless he proves that the statement was made with 'actual malice'—that is, with knowledge that it was false or with reckless disregard of whether it was false or not." Next there occurred the extension of the *New York Times* rule to *public figures,* as we saw in the *Hill* and *Spahn* cases, which were right of privacy cases. The New York Supreme Court in a defamation case decided in November, 1969 (*Bavarian Motor v. Manchester*),[31b] was called upon to rule on the sufficiency of a complaint in which the publisher of a nonfiction book on the history of the German Krupp family and its munitions works was charged with falsely stating that the German corporation went out of business and into oblivion. The publisher's motion to dismiss the complaint on the ground that it did not allege actual malice was denied. The court ruled that the plaintiff (the motor corporation) was not a *political or public figure* within the *New York Times* rule, which deprives a public official of legal redress for a defamatory falsehood without proof that the lie was a knowing one or was uttered in reckless disregard of the truth. The court noted that the rule had been extended to public figures in the *Hill* case, but refused to extend it further to include the plaintiff corporation, saying:

Plaintiff herein, Bavarian Motor Works, appears not to be a public person within the purview of the *New York Times* line of cases. Further, the defendants do not make even a colorable showing that it is such a person. Defendants' contention appears to be premised on the argument that the above-mentioned book is imbued with such public interest and furnishes so much information that it falls within the ambit of a "public issue" rationale and thereby deserves the "protection" of the *New York Times* rule. While the dissemination of historical information serves a most laudable educational need, it does not necessarily follow that by the mere fact of alleged libelous matter being contained therein, such matter is entitled to the benefit of the *New York Times* rule. To extend the *New York Times* rule to the circumstances herein would, it appears, be an unwarranted abridgment of private rights in the libel area and might very well be a further step to granting those in the position of the defendants a valid unconditional license, except where actual malice can be proved by the plaintiff. This court, mindful that such result might put at hazard those very rights and freedoms claimed by the defendants, is not about to so expand the *New York Times* rule.

We therefore see that notwithstanding the legal distinctions between defamation and right of privacy, the courts have granted to publishers constitutional protection of free speech and press in suits by public officials and public figures in both defamation and right of privacy cases. In the *Bavarian Motor* case, however, the court indicated that a state of flux prevails in this area of law. Future cases may interpret the law differently, and we caution our readers that competent legal advice should be obtained regarding any problem that a photographer or publisher may have in this area.

Privacy and Property Rights

The right of privacy belongs only to living persons. Deceased persons[32] (except in Utah by statute) and animals have no right of privacy,[33] nor do corporations, and the law is not applicable to pictures taken of private property. Yet the photographer's right to *use* the picture of an animal or private property may be challenged on other grounds, particularly where the use is for advertising purposes. (See the *Ylla* case in the next chapter on ownership of the photograph.)[34] In another interesting case, a famous photographer was sued for allowing the picture of an unusual tree which he had photographed to be used as calendar art and for other illustrative purposes. The theory of the complaint was that the owner of the tree had a property right which was being violated. The case was settled before it went to trial and the court thus did not have to decide the issue. Despite the fact that the plaintiff's theory in this case lacks the support of previous judicial determination, the photographer who wants to use pictures of private property for advertising illustrations should get a release, if possible.

Summary

Before turning to the subject of model releases, we should note once again that the right of privacy is not the same in all states, and that in some states it has not even been recognized by the courts. It can be said that whether recognition of the right of privacy in a particular state is the result of a statute or judge-made law, the same decisions will generally be reached by the courts on similar sets of facts. At the same time, however, one cannot escape the fact that the states which have statutes similar to that of New York have construed the right of privacy more narrowly than those which do not. In some situations, therefore, jurisdictions not having a statute might reach a result favoring the plaintiff where a statutory state would not. These differences between the states—non-recognition of the right by some, statutory development in others, and non-statutory recognition in still others—make the model release a matter of paramount importance. When a photographer submits a photograph to a publisher, the publisher must be concerned with the law of all states where his magazine is sold, not just the law of the photographer's state.

The photographer might well ask where he stands in relation to the use made of pictures that he has sold to publications that find their way into books and articles of the kind discussed in the various cases in this chapter. If the photographer knows that the pictures are to be used for advertising or trade purposes, he will be liable unless he has obtained a release from the subject. However, if the pictures are sold for editorial use, such as in a non-fiction book or in a magazine in connection with an article or item that is newsworthy or of general interest, it is unlikely that he would be liable if the pictures were misused, even though no release had been obtained. Nevertheless, we strongly suggest that the photographer's bill or invoice covering the sale of the picture state that it is being sold for editorial use only to protect the photographer who does not obtain a model release against a claim that he sold the picture with knowledge of its proposed improper use.

Model Releases

There can be no doubt that the photographer is well-advised to obtain model releases from his subjects whenever possible, even though at the time he takes the picture he may not expect to use it for a purpose proscribed by the laws concerning privacy. What kind of model release ("consent" is probably a better word since "model release" is merely the name used to describe the written instrument which embodies the consent of the subject) is required?

Under the New York statute, the consent must be in writing. In states where the right of privacy is not statutory, the consent may be oral. It is always much better, even where a written release is not required, to secure it in writing. It avoids the problem of proving oral consent in court or of asking the judge or jury to decide who is telling the truth as to whether the consent was obtained.

Although the New York statute requires written consent, oral consent may be pleaded as a partial defense in mitigation of damages, but not as a complete defense. For example, in the case of *Miller v. Madison Square Garden Corp.,*[35] a plaintiff had consented orally to the publication of his name and picture. It was also found that plaintiff had not been subjected to ridicule or humiliation as a result of the publication, and that he had suffered no damage. Under these circumstances the court awarded a verdict to the plaintiff for a technical violation of the New York statute: The sum of six cents for nominal damages.

Similarly, the oral consent of a parent was allowed as a partial defense in mitigation of damages where an action under the New York statute was brought by a minor.[36] In still another New York case where an actress sued for unauthorized use of her photograph for advertising purposes, it was held that defendant could plead as a partial defense the existence of a general custom in the theatrical profession under which persons in that profession permitted and encouraged the use of their pictures in advertisements without compensation and without their written consent.[37]

Must the photographer pay for a release for it to be effective? No. All that is required is the consent of the subject. Professional models who are paid for their services sign releases as a matter of course. An amateur who wishes to induce subjects to sign a release will usually be successful by the application of tact and the proffer of finished prints, and quite often tact alone will suffice.

While a model release is the photographer's best protection against right of privacy suits, it is not a guarantee that the photographer will not be sued. The broader the release, the greater the protection. Observe the language in releases A, B, C, D and E at the end of this chapter. They are all standard releases. Release A is the most comprehensive, but some photographers and advertising agencies prefer the simpler forms represented by B and C. Another form of release executed by the parent or guardian of a minor is shown in D. In E there is no reference to "valuable consideration" or "value received." As indicated above, payment is not necessary. Only consent is required, and some photographers may find it easier to get a subject's release if they use simpler language.

Even the comprehensive, detailed release will not prevent litigation in some situations. A good case in point is one in which a New York fashion model posed for an advertisement to promote a book club.[38] The picture showed her in bed reading a book. The model had signed a release for this picture. Subsequently the picture appeared in a different advertisement but it had been altered by changing the appearance of the man also in the picture. Underneath the photograph in the second advertisement was an invitation to readers to supply a caption to advertise bed sheets. The advertiser said that he tried to write such a caption but all he could come up with was "Lost Week-End," "Knight Errant," "Lost Between the Covers," and "You can't go wrong with a Springmaid Sheet." The model sued for $50,000, charging she had not consented to the second use of the photograph and that she had been damaged socially and professionally by an ad which invited readers to make insinuations about her moral character. The advertiser countered that the model had signed a release which was sufficiently broad to allow the owner of the picture to use it as he saw fit.

The written release signed by the model expressly gave the photographer and "advertisers, customers, successors and assigns" the right to use the photograph for advertising and purposes of trade and "waived the right to inspect or approve the completed . . . pictures."

In denying the defendant's motion to dismiss the complaint, the court refused to accept any evidence that the model and the photographer had made an oral agreement that the picture was to be used *only* for the book club ad because of the existence of the signed release. Then the court said that although the release was sufficient to prevent the model from recovering damages for re-use of the picture in its original form, it was not at all clear that it included permission to alter the picture and then republish it, since the waiver of the right to inspect or approve the picture applied only to the photographer's original finished product. This case never reached trial, and so there was no final decision as to whether or not the release did, in fact, cover the second advertisement. The decision on the motion to dismiss the complaint, however, demonstrates how the question of the scope of a consent may be raised and once again illustrates the dangers of altering or retouching a photograph. In such cases the model may well ask a question which the court posed in this decision—is this the photograph for which she granted a consent?

In still another case,[39] where the release contained a statement that the picture could be used "in whole or in part," or "composite or distorted" in character or form, and where the model waived the right to inspect or approve the picture before its use, the model brought suit to recover damages for libel, claiming that the photograph had been published depicting her without her hair in an advertisement bearing the caption, "All Bald-up on Hair-dos?"

The lower court ruled that even though the release stated that there could be a distorted representation, this did not permit a use which would hold the subject up to ridicule and hence be libelous. The publisher appealed this decision and the Appellate Court ruled that it could not be determined from the release exactly what the publisher could do under the clause of the release permitting use of the picture in composite or distorted form. The court said it may very well be that the parties intended that defendant might do exactly what was complained of by the model and that the publisher should not be denied the right to prove that fact. Thus, if the release itself is clear as to what liberties may be taken with the picture, it may well be that the model cannot later be heard to complain.

Note that this case is different from the Burton case which involved an ad for Camel cigarettes and which we will discuss at the beginning of the chapter on libel, Chapter 7. In the "Hair-Do" case the release specifically covered the question of distortion. From the standpoint of the photographer, then, it is best to use the detailed release covering such matters as blurring, distortion, alterations and others (Model Release Form A).

In the most recent case on the subject (*Leslie v. Milky Way Productions*),[39a] the New York Supreme Court held that even where a professional model had signed a release permitting broad use of her nude pictures, providing for her compensation, and waiving any right to inspect or approve the pictures or advertising copy, the burden was on the defendant to establish that the release was given for the particular use made. This was published in an issue of a newspaper called "Smut" in conjunction with advertisements for the following articles: "Guide to Hookers"; "A Healthy Slut"; and "Sex with a Fist." The model sued claiming the pictures were not to be used commercially and were only to be used in her portfolio and that of the photographer who had since died. She denied that she had ever consented to or authorized the use of the picture in "Smut." The publication moved to dismiss her complaint on the basis of the release that she had signed.

In denying the defendant's motion to dismiss the case, the court noted that there was no dispute as to whether the model had indeed signed the release. The court stated at the outset that where defendant relies upon a release as a bar to the action, the burden is on defendant to prove that the release was given by the model to cover the particular use made. The court then went on to make the following comments about the model release which should serve as notice to make certain that the intended use is specified and that other conditions of the release (such as payment) have been complied with:

The release itself does not specify the name of the photographer, nor the date it was executed, nor the photographs it relates to.

Additionally, there is no showing how the defendants obtained the photographs, except for an assertion that they were obtained from an alleged agent of the photographer: Graphic House, Inc. No supporting affidavit is submitted to show or demonstrate how Graphic House, Inc., came into possession of the photographs and whether it did so in accordance with the terms and provisions of the purported release.

Moreover, it may well be that even though the release can be shown to cover the photograph in question and that the agent Graphic House, Inc., properly came into possession of the photographs, the release could still be held ineffective to constitute plaintiff's consent to defendants' publication of the photograph. This result would be warranted on a showing that plaintiff received no consideration for posing for the photograph;

that the alleged agent obtained the photographs from someone other than the photographer after plaintiff refused to buy the nude photographs from the individual. Consequently, the release, if applicable, would be considered a gratuitous license to publish the photograph that was revocable at any time (see *Garden v. Parfumerie Regard,* 151 Misc. 692, 271 N.Y.S. 187).

Accordingly, defendants' motion to dismiss the complaint on the grounds that a defense is founded upon documentary evidence is denied.

Model Release Form A

In consideration of my engagement as model, upon the terms hereinafter stated, I hereby give X, his legal representatives and assigns, those for whom X is acting, and those acting with his authority or permission, the absolute right and permission to copyright and/or use, re-use and/or publish, and/or republish photographic portraits or pictures of me or in which I may be included, in whole or in part, or composite or distorted in character or form, without restriction as to changes or alterations from time to time, in conjunction with my own or a fictitious name, or reproductions thereof in color or otherwise made through any media at his studios or elsewhere for art, advertising, trade, or any other purpose whatsoever.

I also consent to the use of any printed matter in conjunction therewith.

I hereby waive any right that I may have to inspect and/or appprove the finished product or products or the advertising copy or printed matter that may be used in connection therewith or the use to which it may be applied.

I hereby release, discharge, and agree to save harmless X, his legal representatives or assigns, and all persons acting under his permission or authority or those for whom he is acting, from any liability by virtue of any blurring, distortion, alteration, optical illusion, or use in composite form, whether intentional or otherwise, that may occur or be produced in the taking of said picture or in any subsequent processing thereof, as well as any publication thereof even though it may subject me to ridicule, scandal, reproach, scorn and indignity.

I hereby warrant that I am of full age and have every right to contract in my own name in the above regard. I state further that I have read the above authorization, release and agreement, prior to its execution, and that I am fully familiar with the contents thereof.

Date ....

Name .... (L.S.)

Witness ....

Address ....

Model Release Form B

For good and valuable consideration, the receipt of which is hereby acknowledged, I hereby consent that the photographs of me taken by John Doe, proofs of which are hereto attached, or any reproduction of the same, may be used by John Doe or his assigns or licensees for the purpose of illustration, advertising, trade, or publication in any manner.

Signed ....

Address ....

Date ....

Model Release Form C

I, (we) ....being of legal age hereby consent and authorize (client name), its successors, legal representatives and assigns, and the ABC Agency, Inc., ...
New York, N.Y., its successors, legal representatives and assigns, to use and reproduce my name and photograph (or photographs) taken by ....
.... on (date) and circulate the same for any and all purposes, including publication and advertising of every description. Receipt of full consideration of $............................... where acknowledged and no further claim of any kind will be made by me. No representations have been made to me.

....

(Name)

....

(Address)

Model Release Form D

I hereby affirm that I am the parent (guardian) of (name) and for value received and without further consideration I hereby irrevocably consent that each of the photographs which have been taken of him (her) by (name of photographer) and/or his (her) assigns may be used for advertising, trade, illustration, or publication in any manner.

....

(Name of parent or guardian)

....

(date)

Model Release Form E

Date ....

Place ....

I hereby consent to the use by you, or by anyone you authorize, for the purpose of advertising or trade, of my name and/or a portrait, picture or photograph of me, or any reproduction of same in any form.

Name ....

The language of form D may be added to A, B, C or E when a minor is involved. These forms are reproduced at the back of the book for your convenience.

Review

A recapitulation of a few of the rules concerning model releases may be helpful.

(1) Although the written consent is not necessary in many states, it is sound practice to get the release in writing.

(2) The consent of a minor to use a picture is not adequate. The release should be signed by the parent or guardian. It isn't always safe to accept an unsupported statement that a young person is over 21.

(3) The use made of a picture must not go beyond the limits set forth in the release.

(4) The release must be voluntary. If secured by fraud, the consent is not effective.

Finally, it should be remembered that what we have said here with respect to the right of privacy is not intended as an exhaustive analysis of the subject. The right of privacy is a relatively new area of law. Interpretations of the law may vary from state to state and as conditions change, so will the law of privacy. Nevertheless, we are confident that photographers will find proper guidance in the rules which we have set forth here.

New York Right of Privacy Statute

§50 **Right of Privacy** A person, firm or corporation that uses for advertising purposes, or for the purposes of trade, the name, portrait or picture of any living person without having first obtained the written consent of such person, or if a minor of his or her parent or guardian, is guilty of a misdemeanor.

§51 **Action for Injunction and for Damages** Any person whose name, portrait or picture is used within this state for advertising purposes or for the purposes of trade without the written consent first obtained as above provided may maintain an equitable action in the supreme court of this state against the person, firm or corporation so using his name, portrait or picture to prevent and restrain the use thereof; and may also sue and recover damages for any injuries sustained by reason of such use and if the defendant shall have knowingly used such person's name, portrait or picture in such manner as is forbidden or declared to be unlawful by the last section, the jury, in its discretion, may award exemplary damages. But nothing contained in this act shall be so construed as to prevent any person, firm or corporation, practicing the profession of photography, from exhibiting in or about his or its establishment specimens of the work of such establishment, unless the same is continued by such person, firm or corporation after written notice objecting thereto has been given by the person portrayed; and nothing contained in this act shall be so construed as to prevent any person, firm or corporation from using the name, portrait or picture of any manufacturer or dealer in connection with the goods, wares and merchandise manufactured, produced or dealt in by him which he has sold or disposed of with such name, portrait or picture used in connection therewith; or from using the name, portrait or picture of any author, composer or artist in connection with his literary, musical or artistic productions which he has sold or disposed of with such name, portrait or picture used in connection therewith. As amended L. 1911, c. 226; L. 1921, c. 501, eff. May 3, 1921.

CHAPTER III

Who Owns The Picture?

One of the earliest principles established by a court in the area of photography was that the relationship between a photographer and his (paying) customer is that of employer and employee. In 1913 a New York court ruled:

> It is settled law that the ordinary contract between a photographer and his customer is a contract of employment. The conception as well as the production of the photograph is work done for the customers, and they, not their employee, are the exclusive owners of all proprietary rights.[1]

It is the law today that in the absence of an agreement to the contrary, in the usual customer-photographer relationship, ownership of the picture is vested in the customer.

Although the rule that a paying customer owns the photograph was established many years ago, it was less than 25 years ago that the question as to who retains the negative came directly before the courts for the first time. Two cases arose in New York on this point.

In the first case,[2] decided in 1946, a court found that there had been an agreement between the photographer and his customer under which the negatives as well as the prints were to be delivered to the customer. The judge who decided the case also went so far as to say that even without an agreement, the negatives belonged to the customer, holding that by virtue of the relationship between the photographer and the customer a contract is implied in law whereby the customer retains all proprietary rights in the pictures and negatives.

In 1947 a case arose from a situation in which no agreement had been made as to who would keep the negatives.[3] In that case the defendant, a professional photographer, was hired to make photographs of plaintiff and several others. The order was in writing and included such items as the number of prints and the price. However, nothing was said regarding negatives. After the pictures were delivered the customer asked for the negatives and upon the photographer's refusal to deliver them, commenced suit. The customer won in the lower court, but on appeal, the decision was reversed and the photographer was held entitled to retain the negatives. Evidence was introduced in this case that there has always been an established custom in the field that negatives are kept by the photographer. Since there was no agreement as to the negatives, the Appellate Court said that the custom in the field should govern.

However, it must be made clear at this point that although the photographer has the right to *retain* the negatives in the absence of an agreement to the contrary, he has no right to *use* them. Note the language of the court on that point:

> It is true that the photographer's right to retain the negatives gives him no right to use them for any purpose whatsoever, except at the request of the customer. The photographer cannot sell the negatives nor make photographs from them for anyone except the customer. . . . There is nothing inconsistent with proprietary rights in the customer and the holding that the custody of the plates should remain with the photographer. This view would seem to represent the expectation of the parties in the absence of any special agreement to the contrary. . . . We hold, therefore, that where a customer employs a photographer to make pictures of him, the photographer, in the absence of an agreement to the contrary, has the right to retain the negatives. He may not, however, make any use of the negative without the permission of the customer.

The above case was decided by three judges. The excerpt from the opinion set forth represents the views of two of the judges. The third judge went even further. He based his decision not only on the custom of the trade but said that the photographer has not only the right to custody of the negative but is the actual owner of the negative. His opinion says:

> In my opinion a photographer owning a plate or film which, upon employment, is furnished as part of the transaction of taking a photograph for a customer, continues in such ownership in the absence of agreement providing otherwise. As in the process of photography the designated object is produced as an image on such plate or film. The photographer's ownership is subjected to a limitation by which the negative may only be used for such reproduction as the customer authorizes. Difference of such limitation in respect of private and public persons is not involved or considered.

This may be a significant decision for photographers, even though it represents the opinion of just one court in the State of New York, since the right to retain a negative could provide a measure of control not attainable when both ownership of the picture and custody of the negative are in the customer. There are still too many unanswered questions, however, for one to speak with assurance on this point, and it is possible that the advances in reproduction of photographs directly from prints and transparencies may make the entire question of custody of the negative moot.

Another interesting case on ownership of photographs was decided by a Federal court in New York in 1956.[4] The plaintiff, a commercial photographer, was retained by an advertising agency to take a picture for use in a specific advertisement. The photographer delivered the negative to the agency at its request, and the agency proceeded to sell the picture to another advertiser without the photographer's consent. The photographer sued the agency for infringement of copyright, claiming that he was the beneficial owner of the picture, because under existing trade usage there was an implied agreement that the photographer retained ownership of the picture. The court held that evidence of trade usage was inadmissible to contravene the "general rule of law" which vests ownership of a delivered photograph in the customer rather than the photographer.

It would appear that the court's decision was based on the assumption that the relationship between a commercial photographer and an advertising agency is not distinguishable from that between a portrait photographer and his customer.[5]

Under rules generally followed by the courts today, where a photographer receives an assignment from a magazine to take certain pictures for a fee, ownership of the photograph will be in the magazine, unless a contract provides otherwise.

What has been said about the ownership of pictures and negatives where there is an agreement for payment has no application to a case where the photographer acts on his own initiative in taking the pictures.

In a case in 1894,[6] the photographer took a picture of a famous actress and had the picture copyrighted. The picture was published in a newspaper without the consent of the photographer and he instituted suit for infringement. The court held that where the photographer takes the picture on his own he is the author and proprietor of the photo and negatives. The court said:

> But when a person submits himself or herself as a public character, to a photographer, for the taking of a negative, and the making of photographs therefrom for the photographer, the negative, and the right to make photographs from it, belong to him. He is the author and proprietor of the photograph, and may perfect the exclusive right to make copies by copyright.

The court concluded that the photo had not been made for the actress who sat for it and that she was not the customer. The fact that she was the subject of the picture did not make it hers. The court held that the picture belonged to the person for whom it was made and since it was made for the photographer, he and he alone owned the picture and negative. This is still the law today.

There are fringe situations in which an element of compensation to the photographer may be involved without giving rise to the relationship of photographer and customer. For example, where high school students hired a photographer to make a class picture without paying him for taking the photo but with the understanding that he could sell the pictures individually to students, it was decided the proprietary rights in the picture and the negative belonged to the photographer and that he could obtain the copyright.[7]

Another interesting situation occurred in a case decided in the New York courts in 1957.[8] A photographer who specialized in taking portraits of famous people arranged for an exhibit of portraits of prominent architects and sculptors. The photographer requested a well-known architect to pose for a picture to be used in this exhibition, and asked him to contribute $25 towards the cost of the exhibit, which the architect paid. The photographer then placed a copyright notice on the picture and used it in the exhibition. Subsequently the photographer filed a copy of the picture with the Copyright Office.

Several years later the architect purchased several prints from the photographer and turned over one of the prints to a magazine which used it in an advertisement for a commercial concern. This was done with the express consent of the architect but without the knowledge or consent of the photographer. The photographer sued in a New York State court to recover damages for the unauthorized use of the picture. A $200 award to the photographer was reversed by the higher court on the ground that since a copyright was involved the state courts had no jurisdiction; the photographer was told by the court that he would have to sue in Federal court for copyright infringement.

One aspect of this case, however, is worthy of mention in this chapter. The question was presented as to whether the payment of the $25.00 by the subject to defray the expense of the exhibit gave the subject the proprietary rights in the picture or whether such rights remained with the photographer. On this point the lower court ruled squarely in favor of the photographer, saying:

> In the instant case the plaintiff (the photographer) requested Reinhardt (the architect) to sit for her in connection with her exhibition; the photograph was to be used for plaintiff's benefit. While . . . (the architect) paid her $25 at that time such payment was made not for the portrait, but in order to defray costs of plaintiff's exhibit. Under these circumstances, an implied contract must be said to have existed between . . . (them) pursuant to which all proprietary interest in Reinhardt's photograph, including the right of copyrighting the same, would lie solely with the plaintiff, and not with Reinhardt.

Since this point was not involved in the appeal, which centered solely around the copyright phase, we regard the ruling as to the effect of the token payment to be an indication that courts will not divest photographers of proprietary rights in their pictures merely because some payment was made, but will inquire into the purpose of the payment. This is especially so where the photographer claims that a true relationship of photographer and customer did not exist.

In another case[9] the late Ylla, famous photographer of animals, was sued by the owner of a dog. The owner requested Ylla to make pictures of her dog with the understanding that she would select and pay for those prints which she wanted. Subsequently, Ylla's agent sold one of the pictures to a commercial concern for advertising purposes and the picture appeared in newspapers.

While one of the points in this case involved the New York right of privacy statute (which is treated elsewhere in this book) and the court held that the right of privacy statute had no application to animals, the question of proprietary rights in the pictures was also in issue. The court said:

> If, for example, a photograph of a dog happens to be taken by a photographer on his own initiative without any arrangement with the owner of the dog, the owner making no payment therefore, all proprietary interest in that photograph, including the right to copyright the same, lies solely with the photographer (*Altman v. New Haven Union Co.,* 254 F. 113). On the other hand, as in this case, if the photograph is taken at the request of the owner of the animal who pays the photographer for making it, all proprietary interest in that photograph, including the right to copyright it, lies with the owner (*Press Pub. Co. v. Falk,* 59 F. 324; *Holmes v. Underwood & Underwood, Inc.,* 225 App. Div., 360, Supra).[10]

The court then granted an injunction to the owner of the dog restraining the photographer, the advertising agency and advertiser from any further use of the dog's picture.

It is important to remember, as we have shown, that, depending on the circumstances, the ownership of the prints, the ownership of the negative, the right to possession of the negative, and the right to reproduce the picture can all be separate and distinct, and can be divided differently between the photographer and his customer and/or subject, and others. Furthermore, the right to reproduce can be limited to one publication with additional fees for subsequent uses. For example, in *Bakacs v. McGraw-Hill.,*[11] the New York Supreme Court upheld a book designer's claim for additional compensation based on the use of his illustrations in a publication other than the original science textbooks. However, the facts were clearly in favor of the designer who easily overcame the publishing company's claim that the fee for the original publication entitled it to reproduce the artwork in future editions. The court was greatly influenced by evidence that the publishing company had in the past issued instructions to its employees that "when you purchase an illustration, you must remember that its use is limited to one book; if you expect to use it in another book or in a new edition, you must pay an additional fee." The same principles would apply to photographers. If your agreement with the customer says one reproduction right only in a specific publication, then the customer must pay for additional uses. The problem in most cases is that the agreement is not written and it is the photographer's word against the customer's as to whether one reproduction right or all rights have been sold. Therefore, whenever possible, see that the understanding is put in writing.

CHAPTER IV

Loss Of and Damage To Film

During Processing

As noted in the original edition of this book, there was a dearth of legal precedent on the subject until May 15, 1962, when the Appellate Division in New York decided the case of *Willard Van Dyke Productions, Inc. v. Eastman Kodak Company*.[1] The case was appealed again and in 1963, the intermediate appellate decision was affirmed by New York's highest court, the Court of Appeals.[2]

Now for the first time we have a clear and definite expression of judicial opinion from the highest court of a state on the legal effect of the legend which has appeared for many years on the packaged film of Eastman Kodak Company.

In this case, the plaintiff, Willard Van Dyke Productions, Inc., had purchased a quantity of Kodak Ektachrome Commercial 16mm film. Each of the rolls of film was packaged in a container upon which appeared the words "Film Price Does Not Include Processing" and, in much smaller type, the following notice:

Read This Notice
This film will be replaced if defective in manufacture, labeling, or packaging, or if damaged or lost by us or any subsidiary company. Except for such replacement, the sale or subsequent handling of this film for any, purpose is without warranty or other liability of any kind. Since dyes used with color films, like other dyes, may, in time, change, this film will not be replaced for, or otherwise warranted against, any change in color.

The particular film was purchased by the photographer to be used in fulfilling a contract with a third party for photographing certain facilities in Alaska. After purchasing the film, the photographer took it to Alaska and shot his pictures. It was conceded that the film was properly exposed and that if correctly developed would have resulted in a negative from which commercially valuable prints could be made and which could have been fully satisfactory to fulfill the photographer's contract with the third party.

After exposing the films, the photographer returned the film to New York, where it was forwarded to Eastman Kodak's laboratory for processing. It was conceded that the film was in good condition when received by Eastman Kodak, but during the development, a substantial portion of the film was damaged by a deposit of foreign material and by rub marks in such a way that it became commercially valueless. It was further conceded that the damage was not intentional or malicious but, of course, negligence was not ruled out.

The photographer then had to return to Alaska and retake the shots which had been ruined in processing and brought suit for $1,537.50 to cover rephotographing the necessary sequences.

It appears that in accordance with the terms of the legend, Eastman Kodak had reimbursed the photographer for the cost of the film plus processing and claimed that it was under no further liability. This claim was immediately rejected by the Court on the basis that there was no proof that the photographer had accepted the same in full settlement of the claim. The Court held that such payment was merely for a portion of the photographer's claim which was conceded to be owing and would not bar the photographer from recovering for the additional items of damage which were in dispute.

Coming to the important legal points of the case which are of interest to all photographers and processors alike, the Court held that there were two separate transactions here, (1) the purchase of the film and (2) the processing, and since the legend on the package of film expressly stated that the cost of the film did not include processing, the attempt of Eastman Kodak to limit its liability for processing to the cost of replacement of the film and cost of processing necessarily failed and Eastman Kodak had to answer to the photographer in damages, which in this case amounted to $1,537.50.

The Appellate Division said:

> There were two separate transactions. First, there was a sale of film by the defendant to plaintiff. In connection with such transaction the plaintiff was given express notice by the defendant that the price paid by plaintiff for the film did not include processing. Thus, the matter of the processing was left for future bargaining. Then, it was some time after the completion of the sale that the defendant received the exposed film from plaintiff and undertook the development thereof. This other transaction, separate and distinct from the original sales contract, was in the nature of a bailment for mutual benefit. . . .

> There was no written or formal contract entered into between the parties for the development of the exposed film. The film was delivered to and accepted by the defendant for processing work thereon without the statement then of any conditions. Thus, there being no agreement to

the contrary, the defendant, on undertaking this work, was obliged to perform it with ordinary care and skill.

The Court then noted that Eastman Kodak did not claim that it was under no obligation to use care and skill, saying:

> The defendant does not claim it was not so bound. It is not the defendant's contention that there was an agreement exempting it from the duty to exercise due care. Even the terms of the notice upon the label accompanying the sale of film are not claimed by defendant to have the effect of relieving it from such duty. Defendant's position is merely that, by virtue of the terms of the notice, there was an agreement limiting its liability for any damage to the film to the replacement thereof whether or not such damage was occasioned by reason of its alleged negligence.

The Court was careful to point out that a valid agreement could have been made limiting the liability for processing to replacement of the film but that such an agreement did not exist under the facts of this case where the cost of the film did not include processing and no separate agreement was made as to the processing which included a limitation of liability.

We now quote the opinion written by the Court of Appeals in affirming the decision rendered by the Appellate Division:

> The law looks with disfavor upon attempts of a party to avoid liability for his own fault and, although it is permissible in many cases to contract one's self out of liability for negligence, the courts insist that it must be absolutely clear that such was the understanding of the parties. In other words, it must be plainly and precisely provided that "limitation of liability extends to negligence or other fault of the party attempting to shed his ordinary responsibility." . . . In line with this principle, we have consistently decided that contracts will not be construed to absolve a party from, or indemnify him against, his own negligence, unless such intention is expressed in unequivocal terms.

The Court of Appeals then concluded, and this may be regarded as the holding of the case, that where the limitation of liability is on the package of film and the price of the film does not include processing, the limitation is not binding on the photographer whose film is ruined in processing. In other words, the previous limitation at the time of the purchase of the film applied to that purchase only and did not carry over into the separate processing transaction, even though the same company was involved and it had spoken in terms of "any subsequent handling" at the time of the purchase. In the absence of clear proof that the limitation of liability was agreed upon as part of the processing contract, the photographer was not barred from recovering the full amount of damages suffered as a result of the ruining of his film.

While this case has gone a long way to clarify the uncertainty previously existing as to the effect of this legend on packaged film where the cost of the film does not include processing, the question is still open as to the effect of such a legend where the cost of the film includes processing and it can be shown that such a covenant of limitation of liability was a factor influencing the bargain for the processing.

Perhaps a case will arise where this specific question will be presented to an appellate court for decision. However, the language of the Court in the above case indicated quite clearly that the limitation of liability must not only be clearly expressed but the processor must also show that the film was delivered for processing with complete understanding of such limitation. The Appellate Division said on this point:

> Consequently, a bailee (which is what the person receiving film for processing would be) relying upon an agreement to cut down the full measure of its common-law responsibility for negligence is bound to show that the bailor (the photographer) with complete understanding that such was to be the agreement, gave assent thereto. (Matter in parenthesis represents comment of authors.)

Most camera stores and other processors give the photographer a receipt for the film when it is delivered for developing. These receipts invariably contain a legend limiting the processor's liability for loss or damage to the cost of replacement of the film. The photographer rarely reads the terms of the receipt unless the film is lost or damaged and then for the first time he becomes aware of the limitation of liability. Normally a person who signs a contract without reading it is still bound by its terms. However, a receipt is not signed by the photographer and a receipt is not a contract. Therefore, we get back to the all-important question of whether the photographer was aware of the limitation of liability at the time he delivered or sent the film in for processing.

If the processor can show that the photographer was given notice of the limitation of liability—even if he didn't expressly agree to such limitation— the photographer might be considered to have implicitly agreed by leaving his film under such conditions, and would therefore be bound by the limitation. However, this is most difficult to prove and since the law does not look with favor upon such agreements, the burden of proof would be on the processor. There is, however, one reported case decided by a court in New York where the limitation of liability in the receipt was held binding on the photographer. The Court reasoned that if the photographer didn't read the receipt at the time he brought the film in for processing, it was his own fault. However, this was a decision of a lower court in 1941.[3] In view of the decision of the Court of Appeals in the Eastman Kodak case in 1963, we believe (in the absence of clear proof that the photographer had notice of or agreed to the limitation of liability on the receipt) that the photographer's claim for damages would not be defeated by the usual small-print limitation of liability.

There is an unreported case in 1951 in which one of the authors successfully represented a photographer in similar circumstances.[4] The photographer had been engaged to take pictures of a high school girl going to her first prom. He was to receive a fixed sum for the pictures. After taking them, he brought the film to a camera store for processing. He had previously made several test shots with the same film to make certain that there was nothing wrong with the film. The exposed film was ruined in processing and the photographer sued to recover the full price he would have received from his client less the expenses of the film and processing. The camera shop's defense was that the processing was done by a third party and that the receipt contained a clause limiting its liability to the cost of replacement of the film. The photographer countered by proving that he had been doing business with the camera shop for a long time; was well known to its employees; that they often didn't bother to give him a receipt; that no receipt was issued on this occasion; and that when he called for the pictures they gave them to him without even asking for a receipt. The Court accepted the photographer's version of the facts and awarded him judgment of the full amount claimed. Unfortunately, the Court did not write any legal opinion which might serve as a precedent for later cases.

One further point should be noted before leaving this subject. The Courts have repeatedly held that such a limitation of liability must be strictly construed against the party who prepared the receipt. In the Eastman Kodak case, the Appellate Division said:

> The terms must be strictly construed . . . and most strongly against the defendant, it being defendant's draftsmanship paring down the ordinary rights of its customers. . . .
>
> Inasmuch as the parties were then contracting with reference to the sale of film, with processing expressly excluded, the statements in the notice, strictly construed, are referrable only to the warranties and liabilities in connection with the sale of the unexposed film. The provision for the limitation of defendant's liability in connection with the subsequent handling of the film for any purpose; would be confined to a limitation of liability in the subsequent handling of the unexposed film for any purpose in connection with the sale. Moreover the word "handling" used in connection with the unexposed film, narrowly construed, would not include processing, involving as it does, more than the mere handling of such film, namely, specialized work on exposed film with the use of materials and technical equipment. If the defendant had intended to broaden the scope of the limiting provisions to embrace liability in connection with such work, we may infer that it would have used the words "development" or "processing" which are terms readily understood in the field of photography.

This means that unless the terms of the limitation of liability are clear that it is intended to cover the type of claim involved, the question of whether or not the photographer had notice of the terms could be immaterial. For example, if the limitation of liability in the receipt covers damage in processing, it will not be deemed to include a claim for loss of film in processing.

It can therefore be readily seen that many complex legal questions enter into the field of the photographer-processor relationship and that, in the final analysis, the answer depends on the facts in each particular case except for situations which clearly fall within the pattern of the cases discussed in this chapter.

Undeveloped Film Lost in Transit

In a decision handed down by the New York Supreme Court in 1950[5] and upheld on appeal by the Appellate Division, a professional photographer recovered over $4,000 in a judgment against Railway Express Agency for the loss of exposed but undeveloped film. Forty-three sheets of color film contained in a package were delivered to Railway Express for shipment to Eastman Kodak Company. They were lost en route. The photographer insured the film for $5,000 and paid the required premium. The exposures were made of scenes which the photographer took during a long trip through the western part of the United States for that express purpose. He was a free-lance photographer and the scenes were shot for sale to prospective customers, mainly calendar manufacturers.

The case was unusual in that there were no legal precedents. Railway Express claimed that even though the film was insured for $5,000, the plaintiff's recovery must be limited to the actual value of the film, and that unless the plaintiff could prove that the undeveloped film had a value, all they had to pay was the purchase cost of new film.

However, the photographer was able to prove all the necessary elements of his case. He proved that he had previously made test shots from film with the same emulsion number which had been processed satisfactorily. He proved that he had used due care and skill in taking the pictures. He subpoenaed the records of Eastman Kodak Company, showing that previous processing done for him over a period of four years had been satisfactory and that the quantity of defective film was infinitesimal. Market value of the lost film was established through records of the photographer showing prior sales of similar pictures.

This case preceded the Willard Van Dyke case in recognizing that the value of film comes into existence the moment the photographer takes his shot, and not when the film is later successfully developed. It was the first case we know of where a substantial value was fixed by a court on undeveloped film. The actual decision of the court was very brief, however, and did not discuss the fine legal points involved.

Here again it must be noted that the relationship between the owner of the film (the bailor) and the carrier (like the processor, a bailee) is fixed by contract. The sender is requested to declare a value on the shipment. Naturally, if you declare a value of $50, that is the most you will get if there is a loss in transit. Therefore, the photographer must be careful when sending his film anywhere to make sure that a proper value is placed on it. It costs a little extra for the added value, but will be well worth it in the event of loss.

Finished Pictures Lost in Transit

Where you are shipping pictures (as distinguished from undeveloped film), the same legal principles set forth above apply. The case is simpler in that you do not have to prove that the film was not defective, that the pictures were properly exposed, and that in all probability you would have had good pictures.

The proof of damages is the same as that involved in exposed but undeveloped film. You must prove the value of the pictures. Value is fixed at either market value or intrinsic value. If the pictures do not have a market value, then you are entitled to recover the intrinsic value. In the Railway Express case the photographer produced records of previous sales of similar pictures from which a market value could be fixed. He was able to show that he sold a certain percentage of all pictures taken by him and proved the price of his average sale. The court applied the same percentage to the 43 lost transparencies and awarded the average price for each of the pictures within the allowable percentage.

But suppose the photographer cannot prove market value. What happens then? In 1900, a case was decided in New York involving the loss of a box of negatives of scenery taken in a foreign land and having no market value.[6] The court said:

> That those articles had no market value was quite clearly shown, and when that appeared the plaintiff was at liberty to give such other evidence as would assist the jury to assess the actual value. That was to be done by showing the nature of the property; the cost of obtaining the photographs; the purpose for which they were procured, and the difficulty of replacing them. The jury were also entitled to take into consideration the value of the property to the plaintiff. . . .
>
> The fact that the negatives were not good ones, and were not well taken, was, of course, to be considered; but, in addition to that, the jury might also consider that when one has gone a long way to obtain photographs of the scenery of a foreign land which is difficult to reach, or where the photograph is of some incident which is not likely to be repeated, even a poor representation may be of considerable value, if a picture can be printed from it, because, as far as it goes, it is a correct representation of what occurred. All of these things were to be considered by the jury. We cannot say that the amount of the verdict which they rendered was improper.

From this decision, which is still the law, it may be observed that where the pictures have no market value, no rule can be laid down as to how the court will fix value. Each case depends on its own facts and all of the circumstances will be considered in arriving at a fair amount.

Pictures Submitted to Magazines

Where a magazine publishes the conditions under which it will receive pictures, the conditions will generally be binding upon the photographer who voluntarily submits his pictures to the magazine. If the magazine states that pictures are not returnable or that the publication will not be responsible for loss of the pictures, it can generally be stated that the photographer will have no legal remedy. Most magazines carry disclaimers of liability or limit their liability on contributions voluntarily submitted (that is, not submitted pursuant to a specific contract between author or photographer and publisher). In the absence of such a limitation of liability statement, a photographer who can prove that a publication actually received his pictures could recover the value of his pictures if lost, unless the publication could show that the loss was not due to its carelessness or negligence. In this connection the photographer is referred to the rules governing legal proof of value discussed earlier in this chapter.

When a photographer submits pictures to a contest, the rules of the contest will generally determine the extent of the obligation of the person sponsoring the contest in the event pictures are lost or damaged.

Pictures Submitted to Prospective Purchasers

Under the Uniform Commercial Code, adopted throughout the United States, in the absence of a special agreement regarding returns, the risk of loss or damage to goods sold on approval (which would include pictures) does not fall upon the purchaser until acceptance (U.C.C. 2-327). It thus becomes important for the photographer who submits pictures on approval to include specific instructions for their return if not purchased—including a time limit and a method of return, such as registered mail, messenger, railway or air express—and to insure them at a stated value. The law says that after notification by the purchaser of his election to return, such return is at the seller's risk and expense, but the purchaser must follow any reasonable instructions. The instructions for return should be in writing and, if possible, set forth in a receipt, which the photographer should obtain for the pictures. It should be noted that although the law says that the expense of return is on the seller (the photographer), the parties may agree otherwise; therefore, when the pictures are submitted at the request of a prospective purchaser, the photographer may be in a better position to have the purchaser assume the expense of return and the insurance or even the risk of loss. Many professional photographers in sending pictures to prospective purchasers for their examination, place a "minimum fee" in a transmittal letter so that if the pictures are not returned, the minimum fee will be claimed. However, an attempt to impose liability on the recipient by such a unilateral legend backfired in a recent case (*Animals Enterprises Inc. v. Fabulous Forgeries Ltd.*).[7] The New York Civil Court awarded the photographer six cents for damage to ten original animal color transparencies while in the possession and control of defendant. The photographer sought to enforce a $1000 minimum fee provision printed on the reverse side of his letter of transmittal, which the defendant had never agreed to. The court's decision was primarily based on the fact that "there was no conclusive testimony that the defendant was directly apprised or notified of the 'minimum fee' for loss or destruction of the transparencies and in the absence of such proof, the defendant cannot be held to have assented to the liability which plaintiff now seeks to impose on it." However, the court made the additional finding that duplicate transparencies of the original damaged ones were in fact returned to the photographer. The following remarks of the court should be of particular interest to photographers encountering a similar situation:

> The court is now left to consider the remaining proof regarding plaintiff's damages. In this respect, the court finds as follows:
>
> 1. That as a result of the loss of these transparencies, plaintiff suffered no genuine pecuniary loss.
> 2. That the plaintiff lost no business as a result of not having the original transparencies.
> 3. There was no testimony that these transparencies could not have been replaced, or if they could, what the cost might have been.
> 4. There was no testimony that some or all of the transparencies were extremely rare or truly unique.
> 5. There was no competent testimony that the duplicate transparencies returned to the plaintiff were so inferior to the originals that they were unsuitable for plaintiff's purposes.
>
> These deficiencies in plaintiff's proof compel this court under the facts and circumstances herein to follow the rule that the defendant bailee is only liable for nominal damages for breach of the bailment agreement (*Mortimer v. Otto,* 206 N.Y. 89).
>
> Accordingly, plaintiff is awarded judgment against the defendant in the sum of six cents.

Community standards now apply in determining what is obscene. Harry Reems, who appeared in the sex film *Deep Throat*, was convicted in Memphis, Tennessee, on charges of conspiring to transport obscene material across state lines by acting in the movie. Although there were successful prosecutions against this film in over a dozen other states, this was the first time any of its actors had been prosecuted. (Photo by Tim Boxer Pictorial Parade/EPA Newsphoto.)

On the other hand, the movie *I Am Curious—Yellow* was considered by the courts as not utterly without redeeming social value. The sexual content of the film presented greater explicitness than had been seen in any other film produced for general viewing. Yet, taken as a whole, "it is an artistic presentation of a young girl's search for identity." (Photo courtesy of Grove Press)

Candid shots of people, like this one, are among the most popular type of pictures made by amateurs today. Generally, when used for editorial purposes, they require no model releases. Yet, because of the way in which such pictures are taken, often unknown to the subject, they can be a potent cause of privacy lawsuits. (Photo by Heber Marquez.)

Outside of the possibility of an occasional local ordinance, the photographer's right to take pictures on public streets is clear so long as he does not interfere with traffic or create a nuisance. (Photo by B. Sastre.)

Picture-taking in a courtroom situation is still a carefully restricted matter. Even though photographers contend that today's cameras are much less obtrusive, and therefore less distracting to courtroom proceedings, it is still left to the discretion of the judge to determine whether the activity of photographers would in any way distort or dramatize the proceedings. (Photo by Andrew Sacks/EPA Newsphoto.)

Photographing news as a matter of immediate public interest is not an invasion of privacy. This is a picture of one of the six women who joined a previously all-male band. (Photo by Andrew Sacks/EPA Newsphoto.)

Although Jacqueline Onassis, widow of the late President Kennedy, is a public figure and thus subject to news coverage, the right of the photographer (Ronald Gallela) was severely restricted. In this case of *Gallela v. Onassis,* the Federal Court in New York held that the photographer went "far beyond reasonable bounds of news coverage by his constant surveillance, obtrusive and intruding presence." (Photo by UPI/EPA Newsphoto.)

Of public interest in 1967 was the play and novel, *The Desperate Hours*. The publishers of *Life* magazine were sued for falsely reporting the play to be a portrayal of the experience suffered by the Hill family. Since the facts were dramatized and distorted in the play, the jury awarded $30,000 to the Hills. However, the U.S. Supreme Court set aside the award but warned that there is no constitutional protection of calculated falsehood and reckless disregard of the truth. (Photo by Paramount Pictures/EPA Newsphoto.)

In the case of *The Estate of Ernest Hemingway v. Random House,* the publisher and author of Ernest Hemingway's biography were sued for an invasion of the widow's right to privacy. The Court of Appeals ruled that Mrs. Mary Hemingway is a public figure who had surrendered her right of privacy to the public. Not only is she the widow of a literary figure of world renown, but she herself has encouraged public attention by writing articles for popular magazines dealing with her husband and with events in their lives together. (Photo by UPI/EPA Newsphoto.)

Public figures have little right of privacy. One has the right to reproduce his pictures for informative purposes, whether in a newspaper, magazine, or book. One court said: "Persons who accept high positions ought not to be so tender about the mention of their names, they must bear the white light that beats upon the throne." (Photo of Jimmy Carter by Andrew Sacks/EPA Newsphoto. Photo of Bella Abzug by Diana Henry/EPA Newsphoto.)

News pictures used to report current events, sports, or other items of public interest may be published without obtaining the consent of the persons in them. (Photos by Andrew Sacks/ EPA Newsphoto.)

The law now provides that black-and-white photographs of paper money, postage, or other "obligations or securities of the United States" may be taken and reproduced for "philatelic, numismatic, educational, historical, or newsworthy purposes." Furthermore, the distance of the camera from the object, the particular angle at which the photograph is taken (as the case may be for this particular picture), or the sharpness of focus, might avoid the degree of "likeness" which would constitute a violation of the law. (Photo by B. Sastre.)

Photographing a work of art in a museum or elsewhere may run you afoul of the Copyright Law, but making such pictures for one's own enjoyment seldom creates a problem. (Photo by Heber Marquez.)

CHAPTER V

The Nude in Photography and the Law of Obscenity

In no other area of law affecting photography have there been such vast and dramatic changes as in the law of obscenity. In the first edition of this book, we told a story about a photographer who, fascinated by a nude painting he had seen in a museum, reproduced the background and pose to create a photographic work of art. In our story, our hypothetical photographer sent his film away for processing but received, instead of the developed negatives and prints he was so eagerly awaiting, a polite letter telling him that his pictures could not be delivered because of the laws against obscenity. The photographer asked himself why the nude picture in the museum was "art" but a similar photograph was "obscene." Changes in the law that occurred between the first and later editions of the book prompted us to inform our readers in the later editions that the above story (which was our way of describing a common problem that plagued photographers just a few years ago) was no longer true. Since the fourth edition, court decisions have further expanded the area of pictures entitled to constitutional protection.

The problem of processing pictures of nudes or semi-nudes has eased considerably. Unless the photographs are "hard-core pornography" they would, in all likelihood, be processed and returned in routine fashion, without comment from the processor. This is a very dramatic and substantial change, which we will discuss later on.

The laws and postal regulations that render "obscene" pictures un-mailable still exist.[1] Furthermore, the United States Supreme Court has up-held a 1967 law that permits any private citizen to stop mail order companies from sending advertisements that he considers "erotically arousing or sexually provocative," and this surely includes pictures. Some rather strange requests have resulted on the part of persons who have objected to "junk mail" of catalogues containing pictures of items such as girdles and bed sheets.

However, aside from this erotic mail curb law, where the recipient is the judge as to which mail is erotically arousing, the big news is in the definition of "obscene" that has been spelled out by the courts, particularly by the United States Supreme Court. This definition importantly affects what will happen under the many statutes dealing with obscenity. The New York statute, for example, makes it a criminal offense to possess an obscene picture with knowledge of its character, with the intent to sell, lend, distribute, give away, or even to show such picture.[2] The New York law also says that a person who possesses six or more similar obscene articles is presumed to possess them with intent of using them for an illegal purpose. Under another provision of the New York statute there is a penalty for distribution of objectionable matter to children less than 17 years of age.[3]

In the past, the Post Office has unofficially applied the criteria of (1) visible pubic hair or (2) a tendency to incite lustful or immoral thoughts or deeds as to pictures sent by mail. In either case, the picture was considered obscene. Many times the problem of making an ultimate judgment as to obscenity was not reached because some processors of prints or transparencies would not send or deliver any nudes, except those made for scientific purposes.

But the courts have now forced the Post Office to take a much more liberal view, and the processors have tended to follow suit. The dramatic change in the policy of processors of film is reflected in the following informative and interesting quotation from a letter of Eastman Kodak Company in April 1970, stating its position on the delivery of pictures of nudes, indecent posture and sexual activity. In March 1976 Eastman Kodak confirmed the fact that this letter still represents its current policy:

> Our primary objective has always been to handle the property and orders of customers in a manner fully in accord with the law. The Company's withholding of films because of their subject matter is ordinarily justified only when it is likely that our delivery of such films would violate the law. Legal prohibitions of this nature have been relaxed substantially in recent years by decisions of the United States Supreme Court. Pictures may no longer be withheld, for example, simply because of nudity or indecent posture.
>
> As a result our policy may now be restated as follows:
>
> (1) We *should* withhold pictures (whether movie or still), which graphically depict sexual activity, if we do not have good reason to believe in good faith that they are solely for the customer's own personal use.
>
> (2) We *should not* withhold pictures (whether movie or still), even though graphically depicting sexual activity, if we have good reason to believe in good faith that they are solely for the customer's own personal use.
>
> Exceptions to the prohibition set forth in (1) above will be considered when it is clear that the films are to be used for scientific, medical or legitimate artistic purposes. Such matters may be referred to the Legal Department for consideration.
>
> As in the past, these principles have to do with films submitted for processing, the character of which cannot be known to us until processing has been completed. When pictures are received for printing or duplication, we reserve the right not to print or make duplicates, especially in quantity, even though we believe the pictures to be legally deliverable.

> Eastman Kodak Company is not interested in offering its facilities for the multiplication of pictures which are clearly offensive. We may advise prospective customers accordingly, at the same time returning the original pictures to them.
>
> We hope that the above information will be of some help.

Formerly, pictures were withheld, whether or not nudity was involved, if they were considered "dirty" or such as to incite immoral thoughts or deeds, and pictures depicting sexual activity were definitely withheld. This has changed, except for that class of pictures depicting sexual/and other activity that falls into the category of hard-core pornography.

The pendulum having now swung to the other extreme, it is appropriate to discuss the decisions of the courts during the last few years to attain a better understanding of how far the cases go in defining what is and what is not obscene. Although the United States Supreme Court has taken a liberal view in keeping with the change of attitudes toward sex and nudity, we must emphasize that in recent years several new judges ascended to that court, and it is entirely conceivable that some of the liberal views expressed by the former majority may not necessarily reflect the view of the new majority. It is true that the court generally follows its previous decisions, but every new case is decided on its own facts, and the court is always free to refuse to follow a precedent that it thinks is no longer valid.

To say to the photographer that "anything goes" is far from accurate, and photographers must be warned that in spite of the vast liberalization in the law regarding obscene pictures, the law still does not tolerate hard-core pornography (which, as will be seen later on, is not an easy term to define, although the legal tests for determining it have been spelled out). We shall try to trace the development of the law during recent years to show the gradual transition from the previously prevailing views denouncing a picture of a nude to the present state where even pictures of sexual activity in certain instances are accorded constitutional protection.

For a long time the courts have held that nudity itself was not necessarily obscene, and that the sale of pictures of nudes and semi-nudes does not in and of itself constitute a violation of law. The courts, in making pronouncements on the question of obscenity, have sometimes said that the test is whether the tendency of the material is to deprave or corrupt, whether its motive is pure or impure, or whether it is naturally calculated to excite impure imagination or lustful thoughts. But the United States Supreme Court has said that because suppressing free speech and press (and photographs are surely included here) involves an important guarantee of the First Amendment, the definitions used in the statutes which make any form of expression unlawful must be very clear and definite, so that people will know what is permitted and what is forbidden. In a series of cases involving motion pictures, the Supreme Court declared that such standards for restraint or punishment as "sexual immorality,"[4] "immoral,"[5] "harmful,"[6] and "prejudicial to the best interests of the people of said City"[7] are too vague and uncertain to be used in deciding whether or not a motion picture could, under the Constitution, be withheld from the public. In *Roth v. United States,* a 1957 case involving the sale of allegedly obscene books and phonograph records, the Supreme Court stated what it thought was the proper definition for the kind of material that could properly be excluded from the protection afforded free speech and press under the First Amendment to the Constitution of the United States.[8] The Court said that the test of obscenity is:

> Whether to the average person, applying contemporary standards, the dominant theme of the material taken as a whole appeals to prurient interest.

As we shall see, however, this definition has been considerably expanded and broadened in the past 13 years.

In 1961, the Supreme Court spoke again on the definition of obscenity, clarifying, in an opinion by Justice Harlan, the definition handed down in Roth.[9] The case, *Manual v. Day,* involved a ruling of the Post Office Department, sustained both by the District Court and the Court of Appeals, barring from the mails a shipment of magazines containing the photographs of nude, or near-nude male models, together with the models' names and addresses. The Supreme Court reversed the decision of the lower courts, and Justice Harlan said:

> . . . The question whether these magazines are "obscene," as it was decided below and argued before us, was thought to depend solely on a determination as to the relevant "audience" in terms of which their "prurient interest" appeal should be judged. This view of the obscenity issue evidently stemmed from the belief that in *Roth v. United States,* 354 U.S. 476, 480, this Court established the following *single* test for determining whether challenged material is obscene: "whether to the average person, applying contemporary community standards, the dominant theme of the material taken as a whole appeals to prurient interest." . . . On this basis the Court of Appeals, rejecting the petitioners' contention that the "prurient interest" appeal of the magazines should be judged in terms of their likely impact on the "average person," even though not a likely recipient of the magazines, held that the administrative finding respecting their impact on the "average homosexual" sufficed to establish the Government's case as to their obscenity.
>
> We do not reach the question thus thought below to be dispositive on this aspect of the case. For we find lacking in these magazines an element which, no less than "prurient interest," is essential to a valid determination of obscenity. . . . These magazines cannot be deemed so offensive on their face as to affront current community standards of decency—a quality that we shall hereafter refer to as "patent offensiveness" or "indecency." Lacking that quality, the magazines cannot be deemed legally "obscene" and we need not consider the question of the proper "audience" by which their "prurient interest" appeal should be judged. . . .

Obscenity under the federal statute requires proof of two distinct elements: (1) patent offensiveness; and (2) "prurient interest" appeal. Both must conjoin before challenged material can be found "obscene" under §1461." ...

To consider that the "obscenity" exception in "the area of constitutionally protected speech or press," *Roth,* at 485, does not require any determination as to the patent offensiveness of the material itself might well put the American public in jeopardy of being denied access to many worthwhile works in literature, science, or art. For one would not have to travel far even among the acknowledged masterpieces in any of these fields to find works whose "dominant theme" might, not beyond reason, be claimed to appeal to the "prurient interest" of the reader or observer. We decline to attribute to Congress any such quixotic and deadening purpose as would bar from the mails all material, not patently offensive, which stimulates impure desires relating to sex.

From the above you can see that a picture is not obscene merely because it portrays a nude, male or female, or merely because it may lead to "impure sexual thoughts." It must be "patently offensive" and "the dominant theme of the material taken as a whole" must appeal to "prurient interest" of the average person, applying contemporary standards. The Supreme Court in that case, however, refused to decide two questions: whether the particular "audience" to which a publication is addressed should determine what standards should be applied, and whether these two tests limit "obscene" material to hard-core pornography only. Let us talk a moment about the second question. "Hard-core pornography" has sometimes been described as material with "prurient" or sexual interest which is so clearly offensive and candid that it would be termed "lewd" or "dirty" no matter what set of "contemporary community standards" was applied. Some courts have said that the Supreme Court definitions of obscenity, properly interpreted, have indeed limited the powers of the courts to restrict, on the basis of "obscenity," only hard-core pornography.[10] This statement has not been universally accepted, however, and it can be expected that some courts (and some prosecutors) will continue to find "obscene" certain material which does not *quite* meet the definition of hard-core pornography. For this reason, although most nude photographs should be considered freely mailable, processors may be justified in refusing to handle material which borders on the pornographic.

If we return to the first question we mentioned as not having been decided by the Supreme Court in the *Manual v. Day* case, we will be talking about a matter which has received considerable attention from the courts in the past, and which has been important in determining whether a particular expression, literary or photographic, could be seized (or the authors or distributors punished) because it was "immoral" or "obscene," etc. In one case, for example,[11] the condemned pictures were found on a magazine rack in a candy store. They consisted of pictures published in sets displaying a strip tease. The models were shown in various stages until complete nudity was achieved. The court noted that the defendant was the manager of a candy store who sold sets of pictures indiscriminately to anyone who desired to purchase them and emphasized the fact that this would hardly be considered a channel through which actual students of art usually buy their material. The court commented:

> Let us look at this case with a realistic approach. Here is a small neighborhood store serving the families of the area. It caters to high school children who come in, observe these pictures, purchase them and seek dark corners and privacy to snicker over its contents and pass the pictures around among their friends.

Here it might be noted that under certain statutes, similar to the New York Penal Law referred to in the early part of this chapter, there is a penalty for distribution of objectionable matter to children under 17 years of age. Pictures that do not meet the tests of obscenity in the case of an adult might very well constitute "objectionable matter" when distributed to a minor, thus subjecting the seller to prosecution.

In another case,[12] "frankly provocative" nude pictures were sold in a store specializing in magic and novelty articles but the windows featured art books containing nudes. In another prosecution,[13] some of the pictures featured two or more models in various poses in the nude. They were sold in a bookstore specializing in the sale of cheap books. In still another case,[14] the pictures were purchased at a bookstore which from its window display featured sexy books with titles such as *Free Lovers, Sinful Cities of the Western World, How to Make Love,* and others. The last three cases mentioned were all tried at one time. The court, in deciding against the sellers, said that in determining whether the pictures are obscene within the law, one can start with the proposition that nudity *per se* is not obscenity. But the judge then went on to say when one sees men pawing over such pictures in stores in the Times Square area, it is obvious that their appeal is frankly sexual and that the pictures in question, therefore, meet the test of obscenity.

Anyone who is familiar with the Times Square area at this time, however, is appalled by the multitude of stores, which have mushroomed in this area, that display and sell books and pictures dealing with sex in all its forms.

As we said above, this is the way that cases of this kind tended to be decided in the past—the court would look at the place and at the community where the pictures were sold and at least partly on this basis would decide whether they were obscene. However, in 1964 a decision was handed down by the United States Supreme Court in the case of *Jacobellis v. Ohio*[15] which decided in quite another way the question of what community standards are to be applied in determining obscenity.

The Jacobellis case involved the French motion picture *Les Amants (The Lovers)*. Nico Jacobellis, manager of a motion picture theatre in Cleveland Heights, Ohio, showed *The Lovers* in his theatre and was convicted on two counts for possessing and exhibiting an obscene film in violation of Ohio law. His conviction was affirmed by one appellate court and then affirmed again by the Supreme Court of Ohio. In reversing the Ohio courts, the Supreme Court said that it was holding to the decision in the Roth case that we talked about earlier in this chapter, and quoted from that decision a statement that obscenity is excluded from constitutional protection only because it is "utterly without redeeming social importance."

The Jacobellis case brought into issue whether local community standards should be applied in determining obscenity, or whether there should be some sort of national standard, with the United States being considered the "community." The Supreme Court, in an opinion written by Justice Brennan, said that local standards may not be applied. Justice Brennan said:

It has been suggested that the "contemporary community standards" aspect of the *Roth* test implies a determination of the constitutional question of obscenity in each case by the standards of the particular local community from which the case arises. This is an incorrect reading of Roth. . . .

We do not see how any "local" definition of the "community" could properly be employed in delineating the area of expression that is protected by the Federal Constitution. Justice Harlan pointed ont in *Manual Enterprises, Inc. v. Day* . . . that a standard based on a particular local community would have "the intolerable consequence of denying some sections of the country access to material, there deemed acceptable, which in others might be considered offensive to prevailing community standards of decency. Cf. *Butler v. Michigan,* 352 U.S. 380. It is true that *Manual Enterprises* dealt with the federal statute banning obscenity from the mails. But the mails are not the only means by which works of expression cross local community lines in this country. It can hardly be assumed that all patrons of a particular library, bookstand, or motion picture theatre are residents of the smallest local "community" that can be drawn around that establishment. Furthermore, to sustain the suppression of a particular book or film in one locality would deter its dissemination in other localities where it might be held not obscene, since sellers and exhibitors would be reluctant to risk criminal conviction in testing the variation between the two places. It would be a hardy person who would sell a book or exhibit a film anywhere in the land after this Court had sustained the judgment of one "community" holding it to be outside the constitutional protection. The result would thus be "to restrict the public's access to forms of the printed word which the State could not constitutionally suppress directly. *Smith v. California,* 361 U.S. 147, 154. . . .

We recognize the legitimate and indeed exigent interest of States and localities throughout the Nation in preventing the dissemination of material deemed harmful to children. But that interest does not justify a total suppression of such material, the effect of which would be to "reduce the adult population . . . to reading only what is fit for children." *Butler v. Michigan,* 352 U.S. 380, 383. State and local authorities might well consider whether their objectives in this area would be better served by laws aimed specifically at preventing distribution of objectionable material to children, rather than at totally prohibiting its dissemination. Since the present conviction is based upon exhibition of the film to the public at large and not upon its exhibition to children, the judgment must be reviewed under the strict standard applicable in determining the scope of the expression that is protected by the Constitution.

We have applied that standard to the motion picture in question. *The Lovers* involves a woman bored with her life and marriage who abandons her husband and family for a young archaeologist with whom she has suddenly fallen in love. There is an explicit love scene in the last reel of the film, and the State's objections are based almost entirely upon that scene. . . . We have viewed the film, in the light of the record made in the trial court, and we conclude that it is not obscene within the standards enunciated in *Alberts v. California* and *Roth v. United States,* which we reaffirm here.

The Jacobellis case created problems for some local police and prosecuting authorities in trying to follow this decision to its fullest implications, because it reduced the area of activity for which obscenity prosecutions were possible to a very narrow area. Indeed, Justice Stewart, who wrote a separate concurring opinion in this case, said that he had reached the conclusion, on the basis of the Supreme Court cases, that under the First and Fourteenth Amendments, criminal obscenity laws are constitutionally limited to hard-core pornography. As will be seen later in this chapter, the law has undergone a change. Community standards now apply in determining what is obscene.

Within five years following the Jacobellis case, a dramatic change had occurred in the law of obscenity. We find a good discussion of the law in a decision of the New York Criminal Court handed down in January, 1969, in the case of *People v. Stabile.*[16] The defendants were charged with selling obscene magazines containing single photographs of females in various poses and stages of nudity, some provocative and prominently displaying the vaginal aperture but not depicting any sexual activity. The court held that the magazines were protected by the First and Fourteenth Amendments of the United States Constitution (freedom of press) in the absence of violation of laws concerning protection of juveniles (a state may constitutionally establish two standards of obscenity, one for minors and one for adults), or in the absence of foisting such material on an unwilling public or resorting to "pandering" methods in distribution.

Judge Ringel's opinion in the *Stabile* case contains such an excellent discussion of the law that we quote it practically in its entirety as follows:

There are two judicially approved tests for obscenity—the Federal test, and the New York State test.

A. The Federal Test

The Federal test, sometimes called the "prurient interest" or "Roth" test (*Roth v. United States,* supra) applied in the Federal courts, fixes the *minimum* standards that a state may employ in judging publications for obscenity.

This test provided ". . . whether to the average person, applying contemporary community standards, the dominant theme of the material taken as a whole appeals to prurient interest" (*Roth,* ibid at p. 489, 77 S.Ct. 1304, at p. 1311).

The test was amended in 1966 in three cases, *Ginzburg v. United States* (383 U.S. 463, 86 S.Ct. 942, 16 L.Ed. 2d 31), *Mishkin v. New York*, 383 U.S. 502, 86 Ct. 958, 16 L.Ed. 2d 56 and the *"Fanny Hill"* case, *A Book Named "John Cleland's Memoirs of a Woman of Pleasure" v. Attorney General of Massachusetts* (383 U.S. 413, 86 S.Ct. 975, 16 L.Ed. 2d 1).

In *Ginzburg,* the Court held that when an objective examination of the material in question fails to establish obscenity, then the Court may examine into the publisher's intent and in that connection may consider the advertising material he issued in connection with the material under review. If the publisher attempted to "titillate" the sexual interests of the public in an effort to sell his product, then the Courts may consider his advertising "at its face value" and declare the publication obscene.

In *Mishkin,* the Court held that a publication aimed at deviant sexual groups is obscene if it appeals to the prurient interest of those groups.

In *"Fanny Hill"* the Court held under this definition, as elaborated in subsequent cases, three elements must coalesce; it must be established that (a) the dominant theme of the material taken as a whole appeals to a prurient interest in sex; (b) the material is patently offensive because it affronts contemporary community standards relating to the description or representation of sexual matters; and (c) the material is "utterly without redeeming social value" (383 U.S. at p. 418, 86 S.Ct. 975 at p. 977).

"Fanny Hill" thus modified *Roth* by requiring that a publication must be *utterly* without redeeming social value before it could be proscribed. Nevertheless, if the book was "designed for and primarily disseminated to a clearly defined deviant sexual group, rather than the public at large," it may likewise be proscribed (*Mishkin,* at p. 508, 86 S.Ct. 958, at p. 963).

[3] The term "contemporary community standards" must be interpreted in a parochial sense but is equated with the contemporary community standards of the nation as a whole since the area of expression that is protected is governed by the Federal Constitution (*Jacobellis v. Ohio,* supra, at p. 193, 84 S.Ct. 1676).

"Fanny Hill" was followed by *Redrup v. New York* [1967] (386 U.S. 767, 87 S.Ct. 1414). In effect, *Redrup* holds material to be obscene if it is hard-core pornography, *and* in "borderline" cases, the publication may be proscribed if (a) it is sold to a minor in violation of some local statute . . . *or* (b) if it is pandered . . . *or* (c) if it is foisted upon an unwilling public. . . .

Any doubt as to the meaning of *Redrup* is resolved in *Central Magazine Sales, Ltd. v. United States* [1967] (389 U.S. 50, 88 S.Ct. 235, 19 L.Ed. 2d 49). *Central Sales* involved a magazine called *"Exclusive"* which contained a collection of photographs of females in various stages of nudity, and some of which are posed in such a manner as "to reveal the genital area in its entirety." There was also some suggestion of masochism in some of the photographs. Although the trial court found the magazine to be obscene (*United States v. 392 Copies of a Magazine Enitled Exclusive,*

253 F.Supp. 485), which determination was affirmed on appeal (373 F. 2d 633), nevertheless, the United States Supreme Court reversed without opinion, per curiam, citing only *Redrup.*

In many other recent cases the United States Supreme Court has likewise summarily reversed, without opinion, federal and state court findings of obscenity as to magazines showing photographs of nude or semi-nude males or females which focused on the genitalia. In each of these cases *Redrup* was the authority cited. . . .

The term "hard-core" pornography is an imprecise term. In his dissent in *Jacobellis v. Ohio,* supra, at p. 197, 84 S.Ct. 1676, at p. 1683, Justice Stewart stated ". . . perhaps I could never succeed in intelligibly" defining that term, "but I know it when I see it." However, in a subsequent dissenting opinion (*Ginzburg v. United States,* supra, at p. 499, 86 S.Ct. 942, at p. 957, f.n.3) he set forth what he meant by that term:

". . . Such materials include photographs, both still and motion picture, with no pretense of artistic value, graphically depicting acts of sexual intercourse, including various acts of sodomy and sadism, and sometimes involving several participants in scenes of orgy-like character. They also include strips of drawings in comic-book format grossly depicting similar activities in an exaggerated fashion. . . ."

B. The New York Test

In interpreting former New York Penal Law, section 1141, the New York Court of Appeals held that it "should apply only to what may properly be termed hard-core pornography." (*People v. Richmond County News* [1961], 9 N.Y. 2d 578, 586, 216 N.Y.S. 2d 369, 375, 175 N.E. 2d 681.) Although many people may know it when they see it, the term was never defined by the Court other than to say that the test "may be applied objectively." . . . The test is far less stringent than the federal test which, as noted above, is subjective and consists of the prurient appeal—patently offensive—utterly without redeeming social value elements (*Roth,* supra; *"Fanny Hill,"* supra; McKinney's Penal Law, Book 39, Part 2, Practice Commentary, p. 89).

[4] However, by enacting Revised Penal Law § 235.00 the New York State Legislature has now adopted the federal definition of obscenity as expressed in *"Fanny Hill,"* supra, thus eliminating the single hard-core pornography test laid down in *Richmond County News,* supra.

[5] Under either test, if the material is hard-core pornography, it is not protected. . . . In this Court's view, pictures of nudes, absent any indication of sexual activity, are not hard-core (see *Ginzburg v. United States,* p. 499, 86 S.Ct. 942, f.n. 3, supra, dissent, Stewart J.).

Although *People v. G.I. Distributors, Inc.* (20 N.Y. 2d 104, 281 N.Y.S. 2d 795, 228 N.E. 2d 787) was decided under former Penal Law § 1141, the definition of hard-core indicated therein is significant "Photographs of similar *sexual activity* between male and female, without social justification or excuse, would be equally obscene." . . . In *People v. Noroff,* 67 Cal. 2d 791, 63 Cal. Rptr. 575, 433 P. 2d 479, supra, the Supreme Court of California found the publication *International Nudist Sun,* Vol. I, No. 5, constitutionally protected because . . . "none of the photographs display any form of *sexual activity.*" . . . In the same opinion . . . the Court noted, "The graphic depiction of such sexual activity seems to be the distinguishing feature of the only materials which the United States Supreme Court has ever ruled obscene."

Note also, that in his dissent in *G. I. Distributors,* supra, Chief Judge Fuld voted to reverse, inter alia, because "there is neither indecent exposure nor portrayal of a consummated lewd act." . . .

Addressing ourselves to the *"Fanny Hill"* test, we conclude that the Federal and New York State tests are now the same (McKinney's Consol. Laws, Penal Law Book 39, Part 2, Penal Law [1968], Commission Staff Notes, Article 235 § 235.00). This means that *Redrup,* supra, and *"Fanny Hill,"* supra, are controlling here.

[6, 7] "Sex and obscenity are not synonymous" (*Roth v. United States,* p. 487, 77 S.Ct. p. 1310, supra). Accordingly, absent ". . . a claim that the statute in question reflected a specific and limited state concern for juveniles. See *Prince v. Massachusetts,* 321 U.S. 158, 64 S.Ct. 438, 88 L.Ed. 645; cf. *Butler v Michigan,* 352 U.S. 380, 77 S.Ct. 524, 1 L.Ed. 2d 412"; *or* "any suggestion of an assault upon individual privacy by publication in a manner so obtrusive as to make it impossible for an unwilling individual to avoid exposure to it (cf. *Breard v. City of Alexandria,* 341 U.S. 622, 71 S.Ct. 920, 95 L.Ed. 1233) . . . ," *or* evidence of the sort of "pandering" which the Court found significant in *Ginzburg v. United States.* . . . it must be concluded that the distribution of the material in question is protected by the First and Fourteenth Amendments.

It is to be noted that many courts have held to the same effect with respect to similar or identical photographs as are before the Court. See *People v. Liebowitz* (App. Term, New York State Supreme Court). . . .

[8] What may be "clearly obscene in the ordinary sense of the word" does not necessarily make a publication obscene as a matter of law (*United States v. 4,440 Copies etc.,* 276 F.Supp. 902, 903, supra). It is to be observed that in this case the Court reviewed photographs of women in various suggestive poses which exposed to open view their breasts and vaginas and were "lewder than any magazines heretofore considered" by that Court.

Note too that the United States Supreme Court has held, in a case where the defendants conceded that magazines of nude males were without literary merit and were prepared for homosexuals, that the magazines were not legally obscene as there is an absence of "patent offensiveness" or "indecency" on the face of the photographs so as to affront current community standards of decency . . . .

In summary, the following conclusions may be drawn from the various decisions:

[9] (1) A State may constitutionally establish two standards of obscenity—one for juveniles and one for adults. (*Redrup,* supra, *People v. Tannenbaum,* supra)

(2) The Federal and New York State tests for obscenity are identical.

(3) Obscene material enjoys no constitutional protection. It is contraband. (*Roth v. United States,* supra)

[10] (4) Hard-core pornography is obscene under both Federal and New York law. (*Redrup*, supra; *People v. Noroff*, supra)

[11] (5) Motion pictures, like books, are entitled to the protection of the First Amendment and the three-fold test stated in *"Fanny Hill"* is applicable to both. (*I Am Curious—Yellow*, supra)

[12] (6) The "prurient appeal" test of *"Fanny Hill"* includes prurient appeal to sexually deviant groups. (*Mishkin v. New York*, supra)

[13] Photographs of nudes depicting sexual activity are "hard-core." (*G.I. Distributors, Inc.*, supra)

[14] Sex and obscenity are not synonymous. Thus, the distribution of photographs depicting genitalia (the so-called close cases; see *Ginzburg*, supra, at p. 474, 86 S.Ct. 942), which are not "hard-core," is protected by the First and Fourteenth Amendments, unless (1) they are distributed to juveniles in violation of some statute, *or* (2) they are foisted upon an unwilling public in violation of one's right to privacy, *or* (3) they are "pandered." (*Redrup*, supra)

[15] Also, in close cases, the publisher's advertising "blurbs" may be considered in determining the question of obscenity. (*Ginzburg v. United States*, supra)

[16] In our view, the term "close cases" refers to material, which on objective examination, standing alone, is not patently offensive, i.e., hard-core pornography (*Richmond County News*, supra). More particularly, the term applies to that material in which some, but not all of the three elements of the three-fold test enunciated in *"Fanny Hill"* are present. (*I Am Curious—Yellow*, supra, p. 200 concurring opinion, Friendly, J.)

We conclude, therefore, that while "hard-core pornography" is obscene per se and does not enjoy any constitutional protection (*Roth*, supra), "close cases" are to be adjudged as either obscene vel non, depending upon whether the material violates the tests pronounced in *Redrup*, supra.

This determination is supported by the decision *I Am Curious—Yellow*, supra. That case concerned the showing of a motion picture which depicted scenes of a young girl and her lover nude, sexual intercourse, and oral-genital activity. Although the Court (p. 198) found that "the sexual content of the film is presented with greater explicitness than has been seen in any other film produced for general viewing," [yet] taken as a whole, it was an artistic presentation of a young girl's search for identity. The Court thereupon concluded that, taken as a whole, the film does not appeal "to prurient interest in sex," and "is [not] utterly without redeeming social value." Thus, "it falls within the ambit of intellectual effort that the first amendment was designed to protect." (pp. 199-200) Accordingly, absent the existence of two of the elements of the three-fold test enunciated in *"Fanny Hill,"* supra, the picture was not obscene.

Apparently, mindful of *Redrup*, supra, the Court warned the importers, distributors and exhibitors that if they failed to exclude minors from the audience they would be subject to attack under *Ginsberg v. New York* (390 U.S. 629, 88 S.Ct. 1274, 20 L.Ed. 2d 195 [1968], and if they "pandered" the film, then *Ginzberg v. United States* (383 U.S. 463, 86 S.Ct. 942,

L.Ed. 2d 31 [1966], supra, would be applicable (*United States v. 1 Am Curious—Yellow,* 404 F. 2d 196, 200, supra, concurring opinion, Friendly, J.).

[17] The rule enunciated in *Redrup* (supra) is consonant with the First and Fourteenth Amendments in that it protects the average normal adult in his right to read, view and hear what he pleases. Any other rule would reduce the rights of adults to read, view and hear only what is fit for children. . . .

The material before the Court is coarse, puerile, offensive and distasteful. But these elements alone do not render it obscene under the law or proscribable.

[18] "[T]he price of freedom of religion or of speech or of the press is that we must put up with, and even pay for a good deal of rubbish." (*United States v. Ballard,* 322 U.S. 78, at p. 95. . . .

In view of the authorities cited herein, defendants' motion to dismiss, as a matter of law, are granted.

In dealing with pictures depicting sexual activity we see that the courts have granted constitutional protection to moving pictures of sexual intercourse and oral-genital activity in the *I Am Curious—Yellow* case on the ground that, taken as a whole, it is not utterly without redeeming social value. However, this does not mean that separate photographs of sexual activity will receive similar protection.

In *Cohen v. Carroll,*[17] decided in the New York City Criminal Court, the police seized 48 separate photographs of males and females in acts of sexual intercourse of manifold variety. The court said:

Not mere nudity was depicted in these photographs, which is not now proscribed . . . but provocative, lewd and lascivious intercourse . . . which is [proscribed] . . . .

These respondents were engaged in the business of purveying . . . graphic matter . . . to appeal to the erotic interests of their customers. They were plainly engaged in the commercial exploitation of the morbid and shameful craving for materials with prurient effect. . . . Respondents do not come into court as the champions of a brave new permissive sexual philosophy but solely as salesmen against a background of commercial exploitation of erotica solely for the sake of their prurient appeal.

Notwithstanding the *Fanny Hill, I Am Curious—Yellow, The Lovers* and other cases referred to above, we still find courts differing in their application of the three-fold test in the case of motion pictures. We have seen where Justice Brennan, writing for the United States Supreme Court in the *Jacobellis (The Lovers)* case, held that the "explicit love scene" in the last reel of the film does not render the motion picture obscene.

Yet in *Hosey v. City of Jackson,*[18] decided in January, 1970, the United States District Court in Mississippi held that the motion picture *Candy* was devoid of literary or artistic merit, presenting nothing more than a vivid portrayal of hard-core pornography, and was without redeeming social value.

The court in the *Candy* film case said:

> This film has no discernible theme or plot and involves a disconnected series of scenes depicting sexual gratification in a shocking and shameful manner. The Court certainly concurs with the observations of defendants' witness Dean John S. Jenkins who testified:
>
> The film is in my opinion a series of unrelated sequences in the life of this girl and each of the scenes builds up to the disrobing of the female and then the filming of various forms of sexual activity with her. In my opinion these scenes are clearly designed to arouse what we might consider normal, as well as abnormal, interest and emotions in sexual behavior." (Jenkins Dep. pp. 5-6).
>
> The defendants categorize the film as a satire or a spoof on various aspects of modern life. Such a categorization, however, does not bring this obscene film within the constitutional protection of the First Amendment. The graphic portrayal of illicit, unnatural and incestuous sexual relationships which dominate the entirety of this film leave little to the imagination and completely overpowers or minimizes the presence of any elements of satire.
>
> This motion picture is violative of the tridentated test as enunciated in *Memoirs,* supra, in that the dominant theme of the material in this film taken as a whole appeals to a prurient interest in sex, the material is patently offensive because it clearly affronts contemporary community standards relating to the representation of sexual matters, and the material is utterly without redeeming social value. All three of these elements coalesce when applied to the film *Candy.* It is necessary for one to view the various lurid and bizarre activities depicted in this film and hear the sound effects incidental thereto in order to fully appreciate the obscene and disgusting nature of this motion picture in its entirety.

In *McGrew v. City of Jackson,*[19] decided in December, 1969, the same Mississippi District Court found the motion picture *The Fox* to be obscene. In comparing it with *The Lovers,* which was held not to be obscene in the *Jacobellis* case, the court said:

> The film protected [in] *Jacobellis v. State of Ohio,* 378 U.S. 184, 84 S.Ct. 1676, 12 L.Ed. 2d 793 (*The Lovers*), [was] reviewed by the Supreme Court, which said that the reel involved an affair between a woman bored with her marriage who had abandoned her husband for a younger man and that the last reel most severely criticized simply displayed "an explicit love scene." That nicety of characterization simply does not fit as a description of the lurid and carnal scenes in *The Fox* which so far exceeded all bounds of propriety and common decency by any standards. *The Fox* is a classic case of hard-core pornography wherein sex is pandered solely for profit.

It should be noted that in both the *Candy* and *The Fox* cases there were dissenting opinions by one of the judges, who declared in the latter case:

> Following the precedent set in *Entertainment Ventures Inc., et al. v. Brewer, et al,* supra, I would have preferred simply to rule on the constitu-

tionality of the pertinent state statute and the constitutionality of the arrests of the plaintiffs and of the seizure of the film. We might then have foregone viewing the movie. However, since we have now witnessed the showing of the film, I would express my agreement with the declaration of Chief Judge William C. Keady.

"That the motion picture *The Fox* is hereby declared not to be obscene, in fact or in law, in accordance with controlling decisions, particularly *Roth v. United States of America,* 354 U.S. 476 [77 S.Ct. 1304] 1 L.Ed. 1498, and *Jacobellis v. Ohio,* 378 U.S. 184, [84 S.Ct. 1676] 12 L.Ed. 2d 793. . . "

For the foregoing reasons, I respectfully dissent.

In an earlier case, *Ratner v. Widdle,*[20] decided in April, 1968, the United States District Court in California held as obscene a motion picture dealing with the subject of flagellation, saying:

The subject film portrayed, to an *ad nauseam* extent, the enthusiastic striking of the "bare behinds" of young women with the use of the open hand, cane, paddle and bullwhip, the last mentioned weapon having been applied indiscriminately to virtually all parts of the mostly undraped figure. The performance was completely candid in portraying what was involved, it also reflected a revolting desecration of the human body. It is particularly in this latter respect that it seems to me to go beyond the acceptable standards that govern the three tests of obscenity (and the test of candor as well, if that is a separate guide).

In *People v. Steinberg,*[21] a New York case, decided in October, 1969, County Court of Westchester County found to be obscene motion pictures with such titles as *The Girl from Pussycat, Professor Lust* and similar titles. In rejecting the argument of defendant that every film has redeeming social importance and that erotic motion pictures have as much right to the protection of the First Amendment as does *Chitty Chitty Bang Bang,* the court said:

Non obscene films do, but obscene films are not within the protection afforded by the First Amendment, *Roth,* supra. Defendants further seek a determination that the Supreme Court standards which are, in fact continuously troublesome be set aside in the interests of logic and common sense. This Court feels that the application of logic and common sense by the Courts of this State and nation to questions involving films of this type might well result in proscribing this type of film as well as the other filth and depravity which prey on society as a whole in the interests of a small group of smut peddlers intent upon pecuniary profits. This Court has obligations to all the people of this country and to ignore the exhibition of this type of gross depravity under the guise of free speech in the interest of commercial exploitation would be a dereliction of its duty to the People.

We have thus seen that pictures of sexual activity, when part of a motion picture, are examined in the light of the entire story in applying the three-fold test stated in the *Jacobellis, Fanny Hill* and *I Am Curious—Yellow* cases in determining whether they are to be adjudged obscene.

Motion pictures also use the pedantic approach to the subject of illustrating sexual relations as an aid to a happy marriage, which although not presented in story-type fashion, would also be accorded constitutional protection. Among the recent pictures are *Marital Fulfillment, The Art of Marriage,* and *Man and Wife.* The same applies to books containing pictures on the subject. However, such pictures sold separately by those engaged in the commercial exploitation of erotica solely for the sake of prurient appeal still face the danger of prosecution as was seen in the *Cohen v. Carroll* case.

We have also seen from the *People v. Stabile* case that magazines showing single pictures of females in various poses and stages of nudity, some provocatively displaying the vaginal aperture but no *sexual activity,* have been accorded constitutional protection even though "coarse, puerile, offensive and distasteful."

What the future holds in store for the sex movies, books and magazines that are inundating our society in this age of sexual permissiveness, we cannot predict.

Whether the present liberal views on obscenity will continue in accordance with the principles previously discussed or whether there will be future legislation creating new definitions, we do not know. It is fair to state, however, that there appears to be very little left that is "obscene" under the law short of pictures of sexual activities which do not fall within the protected area noted above.

But we caution photographers not to be misled into thinking that pictures of anything short of sexual activities are safe, especially where the mail is involved. For example, in a Federal court case, reported in May, 1970 (*U.S. v. Wild*),[22] defendants operating a mail order business were convicted of sending obscene matter through the mail. The Circuit Court of Appeals upheld the conviction. The report of the case states the holding as follows:

> The Court of Appeals, Lumbard, Chief Judge, held that slides depicting nude male, seated or lying facing camera, holding or touching his erect penis or depicting two nude males in act of fellatio constituted hard-core pornography. . . .

Those who have the time and means can appeal convictions to higher courts in the hope of getting a reversal; as stated in the early part of this chapter, however, changes in the make-up of the majority of the United States Supreme Court may result in a second look at the liberal views presently existing.

By way of postscript to the *Ginzburg* case referred to in this chapter, it might be noted that a Federal court judge reduced Ginzburg's sentence from five to three years. Ginzburg was convicted in 1963 for sending obscene materials through the mail. The case became a cause célèbre when the United

States Supreme Court upheld the conviction, not on the ground that the publications were obscene but because promotion of them pandered to prurient interests. At the rehearing for reconsideration of his sentence, his attorneys argued that times had changed since his conviction in 1963 and that book shops and newsstands surrounding the Courthouse now sold books and magazines that made Ginzburg's publications look tame by comparison. His attorneys also argued that since the time the Supreme Court had upheld the conviction it had reversed 16 obscenity convictions in which the publications were overwhelmingly more offensive than Ginzburg's (*New York Times,* May 27, 1970).

Over the past several years, the United States Supreme Court's decisions on laws against obscenity have directed states and localities to apply community standards in controlling the distribution and sale of obscene material. So far, no one is sure of how a community expresses its standards and what kind of community consensus would be acceptable to the courts. Obviously, what is obscene to one is not obscene to another.

The enforcement of obscenity laws, therefore, becomes a matter of fragile discretion and very cautious judgment by law enforcement officers of just what a community considers obscene. This matter of discretion and judgment becomes even more difficult when a community for the most part remains silent on the subject.

Communities such as New York City have particular problems in this regard because of the tremendous diversity of its people and the extremely wide range of their opinions. Furthermore, such communities are major distribution points for publications and films of all kinds. Certainly, community standards exist in these large communities, but among those who articulate these standards there is much difference and confusion.

Although the cases applying community standards are too numerous to discuss, nevertheless, before closing this subject, we should illustrate a recent example of what a New York court considered "hard-core pornography." In *People v. Galbud Theatres, Inc.*,[23] the New York Criminal Court held that a motion picture film *Lickety Split* was hard-core pornography and found the theatre owners guilty of obscenity. The court said:

> The motion picture film *Lickety Split* was admitted into evidence at the trial and viewed by the court. It is a four-reel color film. It depicts the adventures, primarily—one may truthfully say almost exclusively—the sexual adventures, of a soldier who is hitch-hiking back to camp after a leave. It portrays explicit scenes of coitus, fellatio and cunnilingus. It concentrates on displays of the genitalia of the participants in such acts. There is no story line except insofar as the sexual adventures follow each other as incidents of the hero's brief journey.
>
> A motion picture film is "material" within the clear language of P.L. 235.05. To exhibit a motion picture film in a theater to persons who pay admission fees to view it is "to promote" it, within the meaning of that statute.

This court determines as a fact that the motion picture *Lickety Split* is obscene; that the average ordinary adult person, applying contemporary community standards, would find that, considered as a whole, its predominant appeal is to the prurient interest in sex; that it depicts in a patently offensive manner actual sexual intercourse, sodomy, masturbation and lewd exhibition of the genitals; and, considered as a whole, it is lacking in serious literary, artistic, political or scientific value. It is obscene by the standard described in article 235 of our Penal Law. It is obscene by the standard described by the Supreme Court of the United States in *Miller v. California* (413 U.S. 15). It is obscene as that term is described by our Court of Appeals in *People v. Heller* (29 N.Y. 2d 319) and again in the same case on reconsideration (33 N.Y. 2d 314). It is hard-core pornography.

In closing, we might add by way of consolation to photographers that most of the prosecutions have been against sellers and distributors of the material, although photographers are not totally immune. Porno stars themselves have not been as fortunate in escaping immunity from prosecution. Harry Reems, who appeared in the sex film *Deep Throat* was convicted in Memphis, Tennessee, on charges of conspiring to transport obscene material across state lines by acting in the movie. He has appealed his conviction. The *New York Times* in reporting the conviction stated that although there were successful prosecutions against the film *Deep Throat* in over a dozen other states, this was the first time any of its actors or principal financial backers has been prosecuted. The appeal is expected to be heard by the United States Court of Appeals (6th Circuit) during the early part of 1977. The *New York Times* article indicates that Mr. Reems is also scheduled to go on trial again in Memphis on identical conspiracy charges for his lead role in *The Devil in Miss Jones*.

And as this edition goes to press, two additional heavy blows have been delivered against publishers of sex magazines. Larry Flynt, publisher of *Hustler* magazine, has been convicted and sentenced to a jail term of from seven to 25 years (which is under appeal). Al Goldstein, publisher of *Screw* magazine, has also been convicted but was granted a new trial because of the inflammatory nature of the prosecutor's summation to the jury. Both cases will probably end up before the United States Supreme Court which, in the *Miller v. California* case (cited above), ruled in 1973 that the obscenity issue would have to be decided in part by "community standards." The *New York Times,* in an article published in the March 6, 1977 issue of the Sunday Magazine, has expressed the opinion that the term "community standards" is an innocuous term which conceals a trap because the Supreme Court in the Miller case did not specify whether "community" meant the judicial district from which the jurors were selected and in which the trial was held, or an abstract concept encompassing what was morally acceptable to the average American.

CHAPTER VI

Copyright

As the preparation of the Fifth Edition of this book neared completion, the long awaited revision of the Copyright Law became a reality.

Years of efforts by publishers and photographic societies have culminated in the revision of the nation's Copyright Law for the first time in 67 years.

The anachronistic 1909 law makes no mention of radio, television, tape recording, photocopying, microfilming, computer storage and various other 20th Century technological advances. The new law recognizes the existence of these developments.

Since the main provisions under the 1976 Revision do not take effect until January 1, 1978, the present law will continue to affect existing copyrights as well as those acquired up to the time the revision takes effect. It is therefore important for photographers to be familiar with the existing law.

Therefore, the first part of this Chapter deals with the existing or pre-revision copyright laws. The second part deals with the 1976 Revision and consists of an announcement recently received from the U.S. Copyright Office which summarizes the major provisions of the revision as well as the text of several sections of the new statute. In view of the limited amount of material presently available concerning the revision, what follows is not intended to be an exhaustive study of the revision but rather an introduction to the highlights of the new law. Furthermore, the new law calls for an issuance of regulations, revised application forms and printed matter to implement the law, none of which has been received at the writing of this edition. Nor has there been time for an analysis of the new statute to determine its impact on the field of photography. Obviously, general benefits accruing to all authors, such as extension of the life of copyright protection from its present maximum term of 56 years to the life of the author plus 50 years with certain transitional provisions, will inure to the benefit of photographers as well.

Copyright Law Prior to 1976 Revision

When photography was still an infant art—twenty-six years after Daguerre's "first practical application of photography"[1] in 1839—the Congress of the United States decided that photography was entitled to specific copyright protection. In 1865, an amendment to the United States copyright law stated that the provisions of the Copyright Act "shall extend to and include photographs and the negatives thereof which shall hereafter be made."[2] From the standpoint of photographers, however, and despite this early recognition by Congress, the subject of copyright protection for their pictures has always seemed a difficult area. One of the problems is that copyright law is quite complex. Another problem has been cost; each separate copyright registration costs $6.00.* If it were necessary to register separately each picture for which protection was desired, this would be too expensive even for the most successful photographers—and all the methods for avoiding the $6.00 per picture charge discussed later in this chapter, involve additional steps in handling the pictures, added legal complications, or both. Photographic societies, as well as publishers in this field, have continued to press for an easier and cheaper, and therefore more effective means of securing adequate copyright protection for photographers.

Why is such protection so important to the photographer? What does it mean to have a copyright on a photograph, and what does it mean not to have one?

Basic Principles

Basically, copyright is that area of the law which is concerned with the exclusive right of authors, artists, photographers and others to use and reproduce that which they have created. When one is entitled to such protection under the law, he is said to have a copyright. To the photographer this means that others cannot publish or otherwise reproduce his pictures without first securing his consent. Such a right must be valued very highly. Without it anyone can reproduce a valuable picture without paying for the privilege.

Common-Law Copyright†

Every picture produced by the photographer is, in the beginning, protected by what is called common-law copyright.[3] Without any copyright notice or registration, the photographer has the right to prevent others from repro-

---

*Effective January 1, 1978, the fee becomes $10 under the new Copyright Law.

†Under the new law the dual system of protecting works under the common law before publication and under the Federal statute after publication is abolished; there will just be a single system of statutory protection whether the work is published or unpublished.

ducing his pictures. This protection, however, lasts only until the photographer publishes the picture, or authorizes someone else to do so. The moment the picture is published, the common-law copyright is lost, and the photographer must be in a position to rely on statutory copyright secured according to the rules laid down in the Copyright Act.

Common-law copyright was defined by New York State's highest court in the case of *Estate of Ernest Hemingway v. Random House Inc.* (also discussed in the "Right of Privacy" chapter), as follows:

> Common-law copyright is the term applied to an author's proprietary interest in his literary creations before they have been made generally available to the public. It enables the author to exercise control over the first publication of his work or to prevent publication entirely—hence, its other name, the "right of first publication."

Many amateur photographers rely on common-law copyright, especially if they have no intention of selling or publishing their pictures, and it is in fact adequate for their purposes, since the common-law right is never lost until publication of the photograph. But the lines of common-law copyrights are vague: the inclusion of a photograph in an exhibit where others are permitted to "photograph the photograph," or distribution of copies to a limited number of people for a special purpose amounting to "publication" for this purpose, can be close questions. The courts have tended, in recent years, to find that such a special purpose "limited publication" did not divest the photographer of his copyright.

For example, in the *Paulsen v. Personality Posters, Inc.* case, discussed in Chapter 2, the question of common-law copyright also arose. The court held that upon the owner's assent to general publication, the common-law copyright terminates. Since there was a sharp disagreement as to the purpose for which the picture was delivered to defendant, the court held it could not decide such an issue in advance of the trial. The court said:

> While submission of the work to a particular person, or selected group of persons, for a limited purpose, and without right of diffusion, reproduction, distribution or sale, would be considered a "limited publication" which would not result in loss of the common-law copyright (see *White v. Kimmell* . . .), there is sharp disagreement between the parties herein as to whether the photograph was sent to defendant for a limited purpose or whether, as defendant claims, it was a completely unrestricted and unlimited submission for purposes of general publication, which would have resulted in a loss of any common-law copyright, which plaintiff may have had in the work (see *American Visuals Corp. v. Holland,* . . .). Since such sharp factual dispute on the issue of publication must be resolved at a trial and precludes the granting of the preliminary injunctive relief sought (see *Morrin v. Structural Steel Board of Trade Inc.,* 231 App. Div. 673, 248 N.Y.S. 273), it becomes unnecessary to consider at this juncture whether the moving papers sufficiently establish that plaintiff in fact possessed a common-law copyright in the photograph in issue.

However, a photographer who has a question about whether a contemplated use of a particular photograph is a "publication" or not is following the best and safest course if he obtains a statutory copyright rather than relying on the common-law copyright.

Two 1964 decisions by the United States Supreme Court seemed to some lawyers to cast a cloud on the continued validity of common-law copyright. One of these cases, *Sears Roebuck & Co. v. Stiffel Co.*,[4] involved a pole-lamp created by Stiffel on which it had obtained a design patent. The lamp was copied by the defendant, which sold its copies at a much lower price. In the course of the litigation between the parties, the design patent was declared to be invalid. The Supreme Court said that federal laws had preempted the areas of copyright and patent and that a state could not, under its unfair competition laws, prevent copying of an unpatented or uncopyrighted article. Since the design patent on the lamp was invalid, the Supreme Court held that anyone could freely copy it. We believe, however, and several lower courts have already held[5] that the Supreme Court decisions in the lamp cases[6] do not have any effect on common-law copyright, because the Copyright Act specifically says that it shall not "be construed to annul or limit the right of the author or proprietor of an unpublished work . . . to prevent the copying, publication, or use of such unpublished work. . . ."[7] Thus, as far as unpublished works are concerned, federal law has not "preempted" the area—has not made it impossible for state law dealing with common-law copyright to be upheld.

Therefore, where statutory copyright is too impractical and costly, common-law copyright may still be relied on. But some knowledge of statutory copyright is indeed important and essential to all those photographers who publish or exhibit their work. Let us turn to a consideration of this somewhat complex subject matter.

Who May Copyright

The owner of the copyright is called the copyright *proprietor*. Ordinarily the photographer, since he is the person who "creates" the picture, will be the copyright proprietor. The situation is different, however, when the photographer is hired to make pictures for a customer. Although the photographer in this instance has been held in some jurisdictions to have a restricted ownership in the negatives or plates, it is safe to say that the customer, and not the photographer, is entitled to the copyright.[8] We have already pointed out in a previous chapter that where a photographer takes a picture gratuitously and at his own expense, he owns the negative and photograph outright. Under such circumstances he alone is the copyright proprietor. Who has the right to copyright can, of course, be changed in any particular instance by an agreement between the parties.

How to Secure Statutory Copyright for Unpublished Photographs

Copyright may be secured for an unpublished photograph by depositing in the Copyright Office one complete copy of the photograph, an application Form J, and a fee of $6.00.* The copy deposited will be retained.

If the work is subsequently published, another registration will be necessary (see the information below concerning published works), along with another fee. If the work is published after registration, the notice of copyright on the copies of the published version should be the year date of the registration of the claim in the unpublished version. If, however, there is new copyrightable matter in the published version, the year date of publication may be used, or, it may be advisable to use both dates.

The first term of copyright is 28 years (in the case of unpublished photographs) as computed from the date of registration. In the 28th year an application may be filed to renew the claim to copyright for a second term of 28 years. (Under the new law there is a single copyright term which lasts until 50 years after the death of the creator of the copyrighted work.)

Securing Copyright for Published Photographs

Copyright may be secured in a photograph when a claim to copyright was not registered prior to publication. Upon publication of the photograph a notice of copyright† on each copy consisting of the word "Copyright," the abbreviation "Copr.," or the symbol Ⓒ is accompanied by the name of the copyright owner. The initials, mark, or monogram of the copyright owner may be used with the symbol Ⓒ in place of the name if the name appears on some accessible portion of the copies. The year date of publication may be included in the notice, though this is not required for photographs (for example, ⒸJohn Doe 1975). The use of the symbol Ⓒ with the name of the copyright owner and the year date will secure copyright in many countries outside the United States under the provisions of the Universal Copyright Convention, a protection which might not be secured by use of any of the alternative forms of notice.

The date of publication is defined as ". . . the earliest date when copies of the first authorized edition were placed on sale, sold or publicly distributed. . . ."

Publication without notice or with inadequate notice results in the loss of the copyright (even if there has been a previous registration). However, if the publication is unauthorized or the omission or inadequacy of the notice is due to accident or mistake, loss of copyright does not result.

---

*Under the new law the fee is $10. New forms will be issued by the Copyright Office.
†The form of Copyright Notice is basically the same under the new law.

After publication with notice of copyright, two copies of the photograph (if desired, to perfect the copyright)* should be sent to the Register of Copyrights, Library of Congress, Washington, D.C. 20559. With them an application on Form J should go and the registration fee of $6.00.† The Copyright Act says that this registration and deposit of copies should follow publication "promptly," but the courts have tended to define "promptly" in a curious way. In the "Merry-Go-Round case" in 1938, the United States Supreme Court said that registration of a claim to copyright 14 months after publication was prompt enough.[9] Other cases followed, and it is now the belief of many copyright lawyers that basic copyright protection can be preserved by publication with proper notice, even though there is no registration until the 28th year of the copyright term. However, where there is statutory copyright obtained by publication, the photographer under the Copyright Act will be unable to sue for any infringements or renew the copyright until he has registered the photograph and obtained a registration certificate. If the Copyright Office should demand that a published work be registered and deposited (which is not often the case), it is necessary to comply to this within three months, or the copyright will be lost and the photographer will be subjected to a penalty.

Obviously, at this point the method set forth in the statute for copyrighting photographs is quite cumbersome for photographers, and can often be too expensive if handled on a print-by-print basis.

Methods of Bulk Filing

Individual photographers and the Professional Photographers of America, Inc. have devised various methods to ease the copyright burden for the photographer such as registering a number of photographs at one time with a single registration application and a $6.00† fee. The P.P.A. plan provided for photographers to assign their literary rights in photographs to the P.P.A., which would make one registration of a number of prints, or of the P.P.A. group of photographs on microfilm. The Copyright Office was willing to accept this bulk filing with a single form and $6.00.† While this plan is no longer available (as the P.P.A. plan has been dropped because of insufficient demand), bulk filing is still a good idea and can still be used by the individual photographer.

One method is to select the photographs you wish to copyright and place a copyright notice on them. Composite sheets may then be made up consisting of a number of photographs on each sheet for registration as published photographs, then the sheets may be distributed or mailed, for example, to wire services, thus effecting a publication. Two copies of the sheets are

---

*The deposit of copies and registration is not a condition precedent to the acquisition and existence of a copyright but is merely a means of perfecting a copyright.
†Filing fee is $10 under the new law.

then forwarded to the Copyright Office with Form J together with a single fee of $6.00.*

Another method is to make up a number of photographs into a "book" with a title page (such as Works or Photographs of John Doe - 1976) and a cover. This need not be elaborately bound (fasteners or staples will do). "Publication" of the book can be accomplished by selling several copies to friends or perhaps by persuading one or two libraries to place it on their shelves, or by selling it in a local book or camera store. The Copyright Office says that if the work consists of a collection of photographs in a book form, the copyright notice should appear on the title page or verso thereof. (See the instructions on p. 4 of Form J reproduced on p. 130 of this book.) The main disadvantage of this method is that a number of copies of the "book" will be needed—several for publication purposes, two for the Copyright Office and at least one for the copyright owner. However, the prints in the "book" (if the pictures are otherwise unpublished) need not be of the quality or size of the unpublished original. The Copyright Office requires deposit of two copies of "the best edition then published" and such a "best edition" can be quite modest.

Life of Copyright

A statutory copyright has a life of 28 years and may be renewed for another period of 28 years by sending a Form R and a $4.00 fee† during the 28th year of the original term. If the photographer is alive at the time of renewal, he (or anyone to whom he has previously sold or given his renewal rights) has the right to renew. If he has died, any agreements he may have made to dispose of the renewal right are invalid, and his spouse and children have the right to renew. If the photographer left no widow or children, then the photographer's executor or his nearest kin will have the right to renew the copyright. The foregoing does not apply to a photograph taken for a customer.

Common-Law Copyright‡

We have already pointed out that most amateur photographers will not take the steps necessary to secure a statutory copyright. In most cases, the amateur will not have to worry about his pictures falling into the public domain unless he places them on public exhibition or sells them. If he sends his pictures to a photographic magazine and they are published, a statutory copyright will be secured by the publisher on the entire contents of the mag-

---

*Filing fee is $10 under the new law.
†Renewal fee under the new law during the first term of the copyright period is $6.
‡The new law abolishes common-law copyright.

azine including the photographer's picture. Even if the photographer sells
the publication only limited reproduction rights, so long as the publisher has
authority to copyright the picture in the publisher's name, the publisher's
copyright keeps the picture from falling into the public domain, and the
photographer still owns whatever rights he did not sell to the publisher.[10]
Some authorities believe (and it is common practice) that it is better for the
photographer to assign all of his rights to the publisher, then have the publisher assign back, after the picture has been published with the publisher's
copyright notice, those rights which the photographer did not agree to part
with permanently. This is one way of making it very clear that the publisher
did have the right to copyright the picture in its name. If it were shown that
the publisher did not have the right to secure copyright in a picture, the
copyright notice on the magazine might not protect that picture.

Exhibition of photographs still involves some risk of a court's holding
that common-law copyright on the exhibited picture is forfeited. However,
decisions in the Federal courts have set the precedent that the court may not
give such broad interpretation to the word "publication" as to deprive a person of his common-law copyright in photographs merely because he exhibited
them.[11]

It should also be pointed out for the benefit of those who choose to
rest upon a common-law copyright for pictures which have not been sold, that
a photographer who seeks the benefit of copyright protection based on publication also takes some risks, and suffers some disadvantages. If his copyright
notice, at the time of publication, is not correct, or if it is omitted from some
of the published copies, the copyright may be forever lost. Also, if he is alive
and he does not remember to renew his copyright during the 28th year, it will
expire. A common-law copyright, unlike a statutory copyright, can go on
forever under the present law*—and the 28-year first term of copyright does
not begin until there has been either registration or publication with proper
copyright notice. As pointed out before, authorized publication *without proper
copyright notice* will, unless accidentally omitted, cause the loss of all literary
property rights in the photograph and neither common-law nor statutory
copyright will ever be available for that picture thereafter.

Assignment of Copyright

A photographer may assign his copyright registration on a photograph.
The purchaser (or other assignee) should send the assignment to the Copyright
Office for recording within three months, since the law protects him against
subsequent assignments by the photographer of the same picture to others.
The fee for recording the assignment is $5.00.† Between the photographer
and the asignee, however, the assignment is valid even if it is not recorded.

*Changed under the new law.
†Fee is $10 under the new law.

An assignment of statutory copyright must be in writing to be valid; an assignment of common-law copyright can be valid even if oral, although it is better to have it in writing. An assignment of common-law copyright need not be recorded. An assignment of copyright registration during the first 28-year term does not convey any rights for the renewal term, unless it is clear from the language of the assignment that the photographer intended to assign renewal rights.*

Copyright Infringement

Subject to the doctrine of fair use, a copyrighted photograph may not be copied or reproduced without the copyright owner's permission. A violation of this rule subjects the infringer to suit for damages on copyright infringement.

There is a vast difference, however, between copying a picture and photographing the same subject matter. A copyright on a picture does not prevent another person from independently photographing a similar subject. Another photographer may even take a picture of a subject in exactly the same manner as did the first photographer as long as the second picture has been made independently of the first. The question is, how do you determine whether a picture was taken independently or with the idea of duplicating the previous picture? The latter is a violation of law, the former is not. The following statement of facts, taken from a federal case which was settled before trial a few years ago, illustrates the problem. The picture of a model taken by the plaintiff appeared on the cover of a magazine. The plaintiff photographer charged in his complaint that although a picture of the same model taken by the defendant was not an exact copy, the model was photographed by the defendant with the plaintiff's picture before him. The defendant, it was charged, had posed the model in the same position, wearing the same costume, wtih the identical color scheme as that in the plaintiff's photo. It was further charged that the defendant's intention was to copy the plaintiff's picture with slight differences for the purpose of making it possible to appropriate the essential features of the picture, thus evading the copyright laws. Had a court found that this was indeed what the defendant had done, we believe that a judgment in favor of the plaintiff for copyright infringement would have been correct.

The leading case on this subject was decided in 1914 and is known as the Grace of Youth Case.[12] A photographer was held guilty of infringement of a photograph he had taken of a girl model. The photographer sold all his rights, including the copyright to the picture. Two years later he photographed the same model with the idea of obtaining a similar picture of her without being bound by the copyright restrictions on the first picture, which now belonged to someone else. The court would not permit such action and expressed itself most vigorously on the subject. The court said:

*New law permits terminations of transfers or assignments; see summary in second part of this chapter.

It seems to us, however, that we have no such new photograph of the same model. The identity of the artist and the many close identities of pose, light and shade, etc., indicate very strongly that the first picture was used to produce the second. Whether the model in the second case was posed, and light and shade, etc., arranged with a copy of the first photograph physically present before the artist's eyes, or whether his mental reproduction of the exact combination he had already once effected was so clear and vivid that he did not need the physical reproduction of it, seems to us immaterial. The one thing, viz., the exercise of artistic talent, which made the first photographic picture a subject of copyright, has been used not to produce another picture, but to duplicate the original. . . .

The eye of an artist or a connoisseur will, no doubt, find differences between these two photographs. The backgrounds are not identical, the model in one case is sedate, in the other smiling; moreover the young woman was two years older when the later photograph was taken, and some slight changes in the contours of her figure are discoverable. But the identities are much greater than the differences, and it seems to us that the artist was careful to introduce only enough differences to argue about, while undertaking to make what would seem to be a copy to the ordinary purchaser who did not have both photographs before him at the same time. In this undertaking we think he succeeded.

As a result of this case and others which have followed, the law appears to be that one cannot evade the copyright statute by the simple ruse of taking a separate picture of the same subject and introducing just enough differences to argue about. See *Tennessee Fabricating Co. v. Moultrie Mfg. Co.*[12a] (U.S. Circuit Ct. of Appeals, 5th Cir. 1/15/70) where the Court said: "Infringement is not confined to exact reproduction but includes colorable alterations made to disguise the piracy."

However, this should not deter photographers from going about their usual business and taking photographs of any and all subjects, animate and inanimate, just because others may have previously photographed them and copyrighted such pictures. The question is one of the exercise of artistic talent. If a photographer exercises his own creativity, in taking a picture, he is on safe ground. If he takes advantage of the artistic talent of another—if he copies—his action is open to question.

Copying can, of course, take place in other ways. One of the interesting cases on this subject involved a copyrighted photograph of a tiger. A magazine made a drawing from the photograph and published it. An English court held this to be an infringement.[13] Thus, a copy need not be in the same medium as the original in order to constitute an infringement.

In this connection, the photographer should note that when he photographs a work of art in a museum or elsewhere (such as a painting or statue he might see in a store window), he may run afoul of the copyright laws if the work of art is protected by either common-law or statutory copyright. As a practical matter (other than securing permission to take the picture from the museum or the person or firm in possession of the work of art), making such pictures for one's own enjoyment seldom creates a problem. It is the sale of reproduction rights to such a photo that can cause trouble. Technically, the painter, sculptor or other copyright owner could and should object to the reproduction itself.

The Highlights of the New Law as Summarized in an Announcement from the Copyright Office, Library of Congress

On October 19, 1976, President Gerald R. Ford signed the bill for the general revision of the United States copyright law, which became Public Law 94-553 (90 Stat. 2541). The new statute specifies that, with particular exceptions, its provisions are to enter into force on January 1, 1978. The new law will supersede the copyright act of 1909, as amended, which will, however, remain in force until the new enactment takes effect.

The following are some of the highlights of the new statute:

Single National System. Instead of the present dual system of protecting works under the common law before they are published and under the Federal statute after publication, the new law will establish a single system of statutory protection for all copyrightable works, whether published or unpublished.

Duration of Copyright. For works already under statutory protection, the new law retains the present term of copyright of 28 years from the first publication (or from registration in some cases), renewable by certain persons for a second period of protection, but it increases the length of the second period to 47 years. Copyrights in their first term *must still be renewed* to receive the full new maximum term of 75 years, but copyrights in their second term between December 31, 1976 and December 31, 1977, are automatically extended up to the maximum of 75 years without the need for further renewal.

For works created after January 1, 1978, the new law provides a term lasting for the author's life, plus an additional 50 years after the author's death. For works made for hire, and for anonymous and pseudonymous works, the new term will be 75 years from publication or 100 years from creation, whichever is shorter.

For unpublished works that are already in existence on January 1, 1978, but that are not protected by statutory copyright and have not yet gone into the public domain, the new Act will generally provide automatic Federal copyright protection for the same life-plus-50 or 75- to 100-year terms prescribed for new works. Special dates of termination are provided for copyrights in older works of this sort.

The new Act does not restore copyright protection for any work that has gone into the public domain.

Termination of Transfers. Under the present law, after the first term of 28 years the renewal copyright reverts in certain situations to the author or other specified beneficiaries. The new law drops the renewal feature except for works already in their first term of statutory protection when the new law takes effect. Instead, for transfers of rights made by an author or certain of the author's heirs after January 1, 1978, the new Act generally permits the author or certain heirs to terminate the transfer after 35 years by serving notice on the transferee within specified time limits.

For works already under statutory copyright protection, a similar right of termination is provided with respect to transfers covering the newly added years extending the present maximum term of the copyright from 56 to 75 years. Within certain time limits, an author or specified heirs of the author are generally entitled to file a notice terminating the author's transfers covering any part of the period (usually 19 years) that has now been added to the end of the second term of copyright in a work already under protection when the new law comes into effect.

Government Publications. The new law continues the prohibition in the present law against copyright in "publications of the United States Government" but clarifies its scope by defining works covered by the prohibition as those prepared by an officer or employee of the U.S. Government as part of that person's official duties.

Fair Use. The new law adds a provision to the statute specifically recognizing the principle of "fair use" as a limitation on the exclusive rights of copyright owners, and indicates factors to be considered in determining whether particular uses fall within this category.

Reproduction by Libraries and Archives. In addition to the provision for "fair use," the new law specifies circumstances under which the making or distribution of single copies of works by libraries and archives for noncommercial purposes do not constitute a copyright infringement.

Copyright Royalty Tribunal. The new law creates a Copyright Royalty Tribunal whose purpose will be to determine whether copyright royalty rates, in certain categories where such rates are established in the law, are reasonable and, if not, to adjust them; it will also in certain circumstances determine the distribution of those statutory royalty fees deposited with the Register of Copyrights.

Sound Recordings. The new law retains the provisions added to the present copyright law in 1972, which accord protection against the unauthorized duplication of sound recordings. The new law does not create a performance right for sound recordings as such.

Recording Rights in Music. The new law makes a number of changes in the present system providing compulsory licensing for the recording of music. Among other things it raises the statutory royalty from the present rate of 2 cents to a rate of 2 and ¾ cents or ½ cent per minute of playing time, whichever amount is larger.

Exempt Performances. The new law removes the present general exemption of public performance of nondramatic literary and musical works where the performance is not "for profit." Instead, it provides several specific exemptions for certain types of nonprofit uses, including performances in classrooms and instructional broadcasting. The law also gives broadcasting organizations a limited privilege of making "ephemeral recordings" of their broadcasts.

Public Broadcasting. Under the new Act, noncommercial transmissions by public broadcasters of music and graphic works will be subject to a form of compulsory licensing under terms and rates prescribed by the Copyright Royalty Tribunal.

Jukebox Exemption. The new law removes the present exemption for performances of copyrighted music by jukeboxes. It will substitute a system of compulsory licenses based upon the payment by jukebox operators of an annual royalty fee to the Register of Copyrights for later distribution by the Copyright Royalty Tribunal to the copyright owners.

Cable Television. The new law provides for the payment, under a system of compulsory licensing, of certain royalties for the secondary transmission of copyrighted works on cable television systems (CATV). The amounts are to be paid to the Register of Copyrights for later distribution to the copyright owners by the Copyright Royalty Tribunal.

Notice of Copyright. The old law now requires, as a mandatory condition of copyright protection, that the published copies of a work bear a copyright notice. The new enactment calls for a notice on published copies, but omission or errors will not immediately result in forfeiture of the copyright, and can be corrected within certain time limits. Innocent infringers misled by the omission or error will be shielded from liability.

Deposit and Registration. As under the present law, registration will not be a condition of copyright protection but will be a prerequisite to an infringement suit. Subject to certain exceptions, the remedies of statutory damages and attorney's fees will not be available for infringements occurring before registration. Copies or phonorecords of works published with the notice of copyright that are not registered are required to be deposited for the collections of the Library of Congress, not as a condition of copyright protection, but under provisions of the law making the copyright owner subject to certain penalties for failure to deposit after a demand by the Register of Copyrights.

Manufacturing Clause. Certain works must now be manufactured in the United States to have copyright protection here. The new Act would terminate this requirement completely after July 1, 1982. For the period between January 1, 1978 and July 1, 1982, it makes several modifications that will narrow the coverage of the manufacturing clause, will permit the importation of 2,000 copies manufactured abroad instead of the present limit of 1,500 copies, and will equate manufacture in Canada with manufacture in the United States.

The present movement for general revision of the copyright law began in 1955 with a program that produced, under the supervision of the Copyright Office, a series of 35 extensive studies of major copyright problems. This was followed by a report of the Register of Copyrights on general revision in 1961, by the preparation in the Copyright Office of a preliminary proposed draft bill, and by a series of meetings with a Panel of Consultants consisting of copyright experts, the majority of them from outside the Government. Following a supplementary report by the Register and a bill introduced in Congress primarily for consideration and comment, the first legislative hearings were held before a subcommittee of the House Judiciary Committee on the basis of a bill introduced in 1965. Also in the same year a companion bill was introduced in the Senate.

In 1967, after the subcommittee had held extensive hearings, the House of Representatives passed a revision bill whose major features were similar to the bill just enacted.

There followed another series of extensive hearings before a subcommittee of the Senate Judiciary Committee but, owing chiefly to an extended impasse on the complex and controversial subject of cable television, the revision bill was prevented from reaching the Senate floor.

Indeed it was not until 1974 that the copyright revision bill was enacted by the Senate. However, that bill, although in its general terms the same as the measure approved by the House in 1967, was different in a number of particulars. In February, 1976 the Senate again passed the bill in essentially the same form as the one it had previously passed. Thereafter, the House, following further hearings and consideration by the Judiciary subcommittee, passed the bill on September 22, 1976. There followed a meeting of a conference committee of the two Houses, which resolved the differences between the two bills and reported a single version that was enacted by each body and presented to the President.

During the period before January 1, 1978, the Copyright Office will prepare regulations in accordance with the new statute and will also revise its application forms, instructions, and other printed matter to meet the needs under the new law. In addition, the Office plans to hold extensive meetings with interested parties in order to make the transition from the old law to the new as smooth and efficient as possible.

Copies of the new statute are available free of charge by writing to the Copyright Office, Library of Congress, Washington, D.C. 20559. You may also have your name added to the Copyright Office Mailing List by sending a written request to the Copyright Office.

The actual text of several sections of the new law with which our readers should be familiar are as follows:

§ 106

Exclusive rights in copyrighted works

Subject to sections 107 through 118, the owner of copyright under this title has the exclusive rights to do and to authorize any of the following:

(1) to reproduce the copyrighted work in copies or phonorecords;

(2) to prepare derivative works based upon the copyrighted work;

(3) to distribute copies or phonorecords of the copyrighted work to the public by sale or other transfer of ownership, or by rental, lease, or lending;

(4) in the case of literary, musical, dramatic, and choreographic works, pantomimes, and motion pictures and other audiovisual works, to perform the copyrighted work publicly; and

(5) in the case of literary, musical, dramatic, and choreographic works, pantomimes, and pictorial, graphic, or sculptural works, including the individual images of a motion picture or other audiovisual work, to display the copyrighted work publicly.

§ 107

Limitations on exclusive rights: Fair use

Notwithstanding the provisions of section 106, the fair use of a copyrighted work, including such use by reproduction in copies or phonorecords or by any other means specified by that section, for purposes such as criticism, comment, news reporting, teaching (including multiple copies for classroom use), scholarship, or research, is not an infringement of copyright. In determining whether the use made of a work in any particular case is a fair use the factors to be considered shall include:

(1) the purpose and character of the use, including whether such use is of a commercial nature or is for nonprofit educational purposes;

(2) the nature of the copyrighted work;

(3) the amount and substantiality of the portion used in relation to the copyrighted work as a whole; and

(4) the effect of the use upon the potential market for or value of the copyrighted work.

§ 113

Scope of exclusive rights in pictorial, graphic, and sculptural works

(a) Subject to the provisions of subsections (b) and (c) of this section, the exclusive right to reproduce a copyrighted pictorial, graphic, or sculptural work in copies under section 106 includes the right to reproduce the work in or on any kind of article, whether useful or otherwise.

(b) This title does not afford, to the owner of copyright in a work that portrays a useful article as such, any greater or lesser rights with respect to the making, distribution, or display of the useful article so portrayed than those afforded to such works under the law, whether title 17 or the common law or statutes of a State, in effect on December 31, 1977, as held applicable and construed by a court in an action brought under this title.

(c) In the case of a work lawfully reproduced in useful articles that have been offered for sale or other distribution to the public, copyright does not include any right to prevent the making, distribution, or display of pictures or photographs of such articles in connection with advertisements or commentaries related to the distribution or display of such articles, or in connection with news reports.

§ 401

Notice of copyright: Visually perceptible copies

(a) GENERAL REQUIREMENT — Whenever a work protected under this title is published in the United States or elsewhere by authority of the copyright owner, a notice of copyright as provided by this section shall be placed on all publicly distributed copies from which the work can be visually perceived, either directly or with the aid of a machine or device.

(b) FORM OF NOTICE — The notice appearing on the copies shall consist of the following three elements:

(1) the symbol ⓒ (the letter C in a circle), or the word "Copyright," or the abbreviation "Copr."; and

(2) the year of first publication of the work; in the case of compilations or derivative works incorporating previously published material, the year date of first publication of the compilation or derivative work is sufficient. The year date may be omitted where a pictorial, graphic, or sculptural work, with accompanying text matter, if any, is reproduced in or on greeting cards, postcards, stationery, jewelry, dolls, toys, or any useful articles; and

(3) the name of the owner of copyright in the work, or an abbreviation by which the name can be recognized, or a generally known alternative designation of the owner.

(c) POSITION OF NOTICE — The notice shall be affixed to the copies in such manner and location as to give reasonable notice of the claim of copyright. The Register of Copyrights shall prescribe by regulation, as examples, specific methods of affixation and positions of the notice on various types of works that will satisfy this requirement, but these specifications shall not be considered exhaustive.

§ 407

Deposit of copies or phonorecords for Library of Congress

(a) Except as provided by subsection (c), and subject to the provisions of subsection (e), the owner of copyright or of the exclusive right of publication in a work published with notice of copyright in the United States shall deposit, within three months after the date of such publication—

(1) two complete copies of the best edition; or

(2) if the work is a sound recording, two complete phonorecords of the best edition, together with any printed or other visually perceptible material published with such phonorecords.

Neither the deposit requirements of this subjection nor the acquisition provisions of subsection (e) are conditions of copyright protection.

(b) The required copies or phonorecords shall be deposited in the Copyright Office for the use or disposition of the Library of Congress. The Register of Copyrights shall, when requested by the depositor and upon payment of the fee prescribed by section 708, issue a receipt for the deposit.

(c) The Register of Copyrights may by regulation exempt any categories of material from the deposit requirements of this section, or require deposit of only one copy or phonorecord with respect to any categories. Such regulations shall provide either for complete exemption from the deposit requirements of this section, or for alternative forms of deposit aimed at providing a satisfactory archival record of a work without imposing practical or financial hardships on the depositor, where the individual author is the owner of copyright in a pictorial, graphic, or sculptural work and (i) less than five copies of the work have been published, or (ii) the work has been published in a limited edition consisting of numbered copies, the monetary value of which would make the mandatory deposit of two copies of the best edition of the work burdensome, unfair, or unreasonable.

(d) At any time after publication of a work as provided by subsection (a) the

Register of Copyrights may make written demand for the required deposit on any of the persons obligated to make the deposit under subsection (a). Unless deposit is made within three months after the demand is received, the person or persons on whom the demand was made are liable—

(1) to a fine of not more than $250 for each work; and

(2) to pay into a specially designated fund in the Library of Congress the total retail price of the copies or phonorecords demanded, or, if no retail price has been fixed, the reasonable cost of the Library of Congress of acquiring them; and

(3) to pay a fine of $2,500, in addition to any fine or liability imposed under clauses (1) and (2), if such person willfully or repeatedly fails or refuses to comply with such a demand.

(e) With respect to transmission programs that have been fixed and transmitted to the public in the United States but have not been published, the Register of Copyrights shall, after consulting with the Librarian of Congress and other interested organizations and officials, establish regulations governing the acquisition, through deposit or otherwise, of copies or phonorecords of such programs for the collection of the Library of Congress.

(1) The Librarian of Congress shall be permitted, under the standards and conditions set forth in such regulations, to make a fixation of a transmission program directly from a transmission to the public, and to reproduce one copy or phonorecord from such fixation for archival purposes.

(2) Such regulations shall also provide standards and procedures by which the Register of Copyrights may make written demand, upon the owner of the right of transmission in the United States, for the deposit of a copy or phonorecord of a specific transmission program. Such deposit may, at the option of the owner of the right of transmission in the United States, be accomplished by gift, by loan for purposes of reproduction, or by sale at a price not to exceed the cost of reproducing and supplying the copy or phonorecord. The regulations established under this clause shall provide reasonable periods of not less than three months for compliance with a demand, and shall allow for extensions of such periods and adjustments in the scope of the demand or the methods for fulfilling it, as reasonably warranted by the circumstances. Willful failure or refusal to comply with the conditions prescribed by such regulations shall subject the owner of the right of transmission in the United States to liability for an amount, not to exceed the cost of reproducing and supplying the copy or phonorecord in question, to be paid into a specially designated fund in the Library of Congress.

(3) Nothing in this subsection shall be construed to require the making or retention, for purposes of deposit, of any copy or phonorecord of an unpublished transmission program, the transmission of which occurs before the receipt of a specific written demand as provided by clause (2).

(4) No activity undertaken in compliance with regulations prescribed under clauses (1) or (2) of this subsection shall result in liability if intended solely to assist in the acquisition of copies or phonorecords under this subsection.

§ 408

Copyright registration in general

(a) REGISTRATION PERMISSIVE — At any time during the subsistence of copyright in any published or unpublished work, the owner of copyright or of any exclusive right in the work may obtain registration of the copyright claim by delivering to the Copyright Office the deposit specified by this section, together with the application and fee specified by sections 409 and 708. Subject to the provisions of section 405(a), such registration is not a condition of copyright protection.

(b) DEPOSIT FOR COPYRIGHT REGISTRATION — Except as provided by subsection (c), the material deposited for registration shall include—

(1) in the case of an unpublished work, one complete copy or phonorecord;

(2) in the case of a published work, two complete copies or phonorecords of the best edition;

(3) in the case of a work first published outside the United States, one complete copy or phonorecord as so published; and

(4) in the case of a contribution to a collective work, one complete copy or phonorecord of the best edition of the collective work.

Copies or phonorecords deposited for the Library of Congress under section 407 may be used to satisfy the deposit provisions of this section, if they are accompanied by the prescribed application and fee, and by any additional identifying material that the Register may, by regulation, require. The Register shall also prescribe regulations establishing requirements under which copies or phonorecords acquired for the Library of Congress under subsection (e) of section 407, otherwise than by deposit, may be used to satisfy the deposit provisions of this section.

§ 411

Registration as prerequisite to infringement suit

(a) Subject to the provisions of subsection (b), no action for infringement of the copyright in any work shall be instituted until registration of the copyright claim has been made in accordance with this title. In any case, however, where the deposit, application, and fee required for registration have been delivered to the Copyright Office in proper form and registration has been refused, the applicant is entitled to institute an action for infringement if notice thereof, with a copy of the complaint, is served on the Register of Copyrights. The Register may, at his or her option, become a party to the action with respect to the issue of registrability of the copyright claim by entering an appearance within sixty days after such service, but the Register's failure to become a party shall not deprive the court of jurisdiction to determine that issue.

(b) In the case of a work consisting of sounds, images, or both, the first fixation of which is made simultaneously with its transmission, the copyright owner may, either before or after such fixation takes place, institute an action for infringement under section 501, fully subject to the remedies provided by sections 502 through 506 and sections 509 and 510, if, in accordance with requirements that the Register of Copyrights shall prescribe by regulation, the copyright owner—

(1) serves notice upon the infringer, not less than ten or more than thirty days before such fixation, identifying the work and the specific time and source of its first transmission, and declaring an intention to secure copyright in the work; and

(2) makes registration for the work within three months after its first transmission.

§ 412

Registration as prerequisite to certain remedies for infringement

In any action under this title, other than an action instituted under section 411(b), no award of statutory damages or of attorney's fees, as provided by sections 504 and 505, shall be made for—

(1) any infringement of copyright in an unpublished work commenced before the effective date of its registration; or

(2) any infringement of copyright commenced after first publication of the work and before the effective date of its registration, unless such registration is made within three months after the first publication of the work.

As stated at the outset of this Chapter, there has not as yet been time to perform a proper analysis of the new law to assess its impact on the field of photography. Photographers will obviously be pleased with the provisions of the law which extend copyright protection for a longer period than that which exists under the current law. However, the increase in copyright registration fees will certainly prove onerous to some photographers.

The following are the salient points under the new law:

a. Photographs copyrighted before January 1, 1978 will have a total copyright term of 75 years (there is an initial term of 28 years and a renewal term of 47 years).

b. Photographs first created (fixed in tangible or copy form) on or after January 1, 1978 will carry copyright protection for the life of the photographer plus 50 years.

c. Photographs created after January 1, 1978 which are made for hire carry protection for 75 years from publication or 100 years from creation, whichever expires first.

d. The life-plus-50-year term for photographs created after January 1, 1978 is not dependent on any renewal.

e. However, the renewal provisions are still applicable to photographs which were first copyrighted before January 1, 1978; thus, a photograph copyrighted in 1960 will have to be renewed within one year prior to the end of the first 28-year term in 1988; the 47-year renewal will then extend the copyright term through the year 2035.

f. Photographs which are already under a renewal term on the date the new law was signed by the President, namely October 19, 1976, automatically had their renewal terms extended for 19 years, to a total of 75 years; the 47-year renewal term is also applicable to pictures whose copyrights will be renewed before January 1, 1978.

g. A cancellation of a grant of a transfer or license of a copyright made after January 1, 1978 is permitted under certain conditions and on notice to be given in accordance with regulations to be issued by the Copyright Office; grants made prior to January 1, 1978 may also be cancelled as to the additional 19-year period added to the renewal term under certain conditions, and on notice given in accordance with such regulations.

h. Photographs which have never been published or copyrighted were permanently protected under the state common law. The 1976 revision establishes a single national system for statutory protection which in effect does away with the state common law. Under the new law, photographs created but not published or copyrighted before January 1, 1978 will be protected for the life-plus-50-year term; but in no event will the copyright expire before December 31, 2002, no matter how long the photographer has been dead; if publication takes place before December 31, 2002, the copyright will in no event expire before December 31, 2027. Photographers who wish to copyright such unpublished pictures before December 31, 1977 should know that if they do so, the pictures will, if renewed, be protected for 75 years. If not copyrighted before January 1, 1978 such pictures will have the life-plus-50-year term of protection. Therefore, in the case of a photographer whose life expectancy is less than 25 years, if he does not avail himself of copyright protection before 1978, the new term of life-plus-50-years may offer a lesser period of protection than the 75-year term which would be enjoyed if copyrighted before 1978.

i. The new law recognizes the doctrine of Fair Use which up to now has been the product of decisional law. The factors to be considered in determining whether the use made of a work is a fair use, are spelled out in the new law.

As with any new law, certain matters will be left to future resolution. The law itself has some provisions which are complex and which will require clarification and interpretation. Should problems arise in connection with the new law, an attorney knowledgeable in this area of law should immediately be consulted.

CHAPTER VII

Libel By Photograph

Libel by photograph is a problem that is closer to both amateur and professional photographers than they generally realize. We were recently told by a photographer that a picture cannot possibly be libelous (at least if it has not been doctored), since a picture tells the truth and the truth cannot be a libel. He was wrong on the first count and not entirely right on the second.

First, we all know that pictures do not always tell the truth. Optical illusions are sometimes created by the camera just as they are by the human eye—a point that was made quite clear by a very interesting case in the Federal Courts some years ago.

In that case[1] the plaintiff was a widely known steeplechaser whose picture was used in connection with an endorsement for Camel cigarettes. Plaintiff had posed for the picture in question willingly and had been paid for his testimonial. He did not, however, see the photograph before it was actually used. By a quirk of lighting, the picture showed the horseman with his hand under the pommel, and the side girth fell loosely in such a way that it seemed to be attached to the plaintiff's middle rather than to the saddle. Looked at in this way the photograph became, in the words of the court, "grotesque, monstrous and obscene," and the legend carried on a second photograph of plaintiff in the same advertisement which said, "Get a Lift with a Camel" reinforced the ribald interpretation.

The court recognized that an optical illusion had been created and that the photograph carried "its correction on its face as much as though it were a verbal utterance which expressly declared it was false. . . ." Nevertheless, the court said, the picture exposed the plaintiff to overwhelming ridicule. It made of the plaintiff a preposterous, ridiculous spectacle and the obvious mistake only added to the amusement. The court added that "had such a picture been deliberately reproduced, surely every right-minded person would agree that he would have had a genuine grievance; and the effect is the same whether it is deliberate or not."

As to the plaintiff's having consented to the use of the photographs for which he posed for an advertisement, the court ruled that this was not a consent to the use of an offending photograph. The plaintiff had no reason to anticipate that the lens would so distort his appearance. The Court would not fix upon the plaintiff the responsibility for whatever the camera might turn out, as long as he did not see and approve the picture before publication.

While the case of the steeplechaser may seem a bit unusual as to its facts, the Court's decision in the case rests on certain basic elements in the law of libel, which all photographers should understand.

A Few Basic Principles

A libel, as defined in the law dictionaries, is that which is written or printed, and published, and which injures the reputation of another by bringing him into ridicule, hatred or contempt. While truth is generally regarded as an absolute defense to libel, there are some jurisdictions which hold that even truth is not a defense if the libel was malicious.[2] Here are some typical examples of statements that have been held libelous by the courts. It is a libel to say that a man is insane, or that he has an infectious disease, or that he is illegitimate, or that he is guilty of a crime, or that a woman was served with a summons in her bathtub.

To avoid any possible confusion, we should also point out that there are instances other than where truth is relied on as a defense where the publisher of a false and defamatory statement has the privilege to publish. For example, congressmen have an absolute privilege in a speech or debate in either House of Congress; and newspapers may report statements made in legislative or judicial proceedings, provided the report is fair and accurate. There are other privileges but they are not important to our discussion at this time. Note also that good intentions and innocent mistakes are not defenses to an action of libel, although it is possible that accidental libel may be considered by the jury in awarding damages.[3]

Applying the basic principles of libel to photography, the Courts have rightfully said that a man may be held up as an object of ridicule, contempt or hatred by means of a picture, just as he can by words.

Necessity of Publication

You may have noted in the definition of the term "libel" that a publication is required. This does not mean that only pictures which appear in magazines or newspapers can be libelous. The term "publication" is far broader than this and includes all types of display. Thus, if a photographer places one of his prints in a showcase in front of his studio or shows the picture to people other than the subject, he has "published" that print for the purposes of the law of libel. Mere possession of a print is not publication. The distinction is important.

Captions on Photographs

One particular area in which photographs must exercise caution involves the captions placed on pictures, for a perfectly harmless photograph can be made libelous by an improper caption.

The photograph of the steeplechaser did not require a caption to make it libelous. But here are some cases where captions caused the trouble. In one instance the words "Fatty Arbuckle's Lady Love" were printed below the picture of the plaintiff. The publication was held libelous,[4] for the plaintiff was a married woman and the combination of picture and caption held her up to disgrace. The Court said that the combination imputed an illicit relationship between the plaintiff and the obese comedian. The same result was reached where a picture of the one-time wrestling champion Zbyszko was captioned "Stanislaus Zbyszko, Wrestler, Not Fundamentally Different from the Gorilla in Physique." The wrestler's picture was placed next to that of a gorilla.[5]

Another interesting example of this problem occurred several years ago when a mid-Western newspaper published the photographs of four school boys under the banner headline: "Slain School Girl Vanished with Someone in Cadillac." Immediately below these pictures, in small type, was the further explanation: "These four acquaintances of murdered Patricia Birmingham are cooperating with police in seeking clues that may lead to the girl's slayer." This was followed by the names and addresses of the boys.

Five or six lines below the pictures, in type five to six times larger than that in the line immediately below the photographs, was a two-column subhead: "Four Youths Held; 60 to 70 Friends Face Grilling." The boys brought an action for libel and the court held[6] that it was a question of fact whether the photographs, captions and heads combined were capable of conveying the meaning that the four boys were the boys held on suspicion of murder. In other words, the question was one for the jury.

Such cases demonstrate the absolute necessity of caution in placing captions on photographs. The photographer *must* ask himself—could picture and caption together reasonably be construed as holding someone up to ridicule? A seemingly innocent caption may often be offensive. For example, one publisher was recently threatened with a lawsuit for publishing a photograph of two women standing close together, one of whom was lighting a cigarette. The other woman was of substantial proportions and appeared to be shielding her friend from the wind. The photographer used the caption "Windbreaker" on the photograph. While the threatened litigation was avoided, such problems need not arise if a little thought is given to the problem in advance.

Pictures Accompanying Libelous Articles

Most libel cases involving photographs arise, however, where the gist of the libel involves an accompanying article or story—not just a caption. For example, a New York newspaper published an article about dishonesty at auctions. Accompanying the article was an untitled picture of the plaintiff who was not even an auctioneer. Obviously, an improper inference concerning the plaintiff could be drawn from picture and article together, and the court said it was libel.[7]

In another case[8] a newspaper published an article about a dancer. To illustrate it they used a picture of the dancer which she had posed for in the nude. The court said this was libel, for picture and story were not sufficiently related.

An interesting question arises in the case of a group picture, such as a picture of a crowd, when the picture itself is not defamatory but the use made of it is, as when it accompanies an article or news item of a libelous nature. Can a person shown in such a picture sue for libel? In *St. John v. New York Times*[8a] (New York Supreme Court), the article portrayed a cross section of personalities who study bound volumes of the *Morning Telegraph* (a race horse publication) in the New York Public Library Annex. One of the persons shown in the picture sued for libel and violation of right of privacy, claiming that the article was an exposé of persons who surreptitiously, without their bosses' knowledge, waste their time in the public library charting race horses and that it described the persons as "drifters" of "seedy" appearance. The court dismissed the complaint, holding that none of the libelous statements were directed at the plaintiff nor was he in any way identified in the picture, saying:

> . . . "In addition, the law is clear that where a defamatory publication affects a class of persons, no member of that class can maintain an action therefor unless it is applicable to every member of the class or is specifically applicable to a particular member" (53 Corpus Juris Secundum, Sec. 11, p. 55). This is graphically illustrated in the case of *Cohn v. Brecker,* 20 Misc. 2d 329, where the court in dismissing the complaint stated:
> "Here the words refer to one not specified of a group of persons. Whereas it is essential that the 'defamatory words must refer to some ascertained or ascertainable person and that person must be the plaintiff. . . . So, if the words reflect impartially on either A. or B., or on some of a certain number or class, and there is nothing to show which one was meant, no one can sue.' *Feely v. Vitagraph Co.,* 184 App. Div. 527, 528" (p. 330).
> In *Vogel v. Hearst Corporation,* 116 N.Y.S. 2d 905, the picture of plaintiff, a young girl not otherwise identified, appeared accompanying a magazine article ascribed by her to be libelous. The complaint there was dismissed on the ground that the words of the article reflected on no ascertainable person. To the same effect see *Hays v. American Defense Society,* 252 N.Y. 266, 274-6; *Julian v. American Business Consultants Inc.,* 2 N.Y. 2d 1, 14-18. In the case at bar, any reading of the article in no way discloses the descriptive language which plaintiff finds objectionable as ascertainably aimed at him, either individually or by virtue of any reference to all of the members of the group. The article in general, portrays a cross-section of personalities who study bound volumes of the Morning Telegraph

Newspaper in the New York Public Library Annex. Plaintiff in nowise is referred to personally or accused of surreptitiously charting horses on business time or of even being seedy or without employment. The article simply refers to "some," "others," "at least one man," "most," and "the hard core" and describes a wide variety of types and personalities. It speaks of "bright eyes, rheumy eyes, eyes blinking into focus behind ashtray-thick spectacles and of striding, shuffling, limping" (Complaint, Paragraph Ten). Manifestly, no one person has all of these characteristics. Nor does plaintiff's name appear anywhere in the article or picture nor is he in any way described in the article. The only identification alleged by him is that it is in the photograph, but it must be noted that he has not seen fit to include it as part of his complaint. Accordingly, it cannot be said that any defamatory publication "of and concerning" the plaintiff has been made in the complaint.

In a libel case (*Freeman v. Columbia Broadcasting System,* N.Y. Supreme Court),[8b] arising from the popular television program known as "60 Minutes," the portion of the program in issue dealt with the subject of pimps and their impact on modern-day society. The script referred to the customized cars driven by them as "pimpmobiles" and the "foppish" clothes worn by them. The script also added: "Almost all pimps are black." During the program a black person was shown driving a Lincoln Continental automobile. Plaintiff, a black who was in the business of customizing automobiles for sale and the owner of a Lincoln Continental brought suit alleging that the telecast was defamatory both to him and his product. Ruling that no defamation of product was involved the court cited another case which held that "it is no disparagement of an article offered for sale to the public—to say that it was bought by a harlot" (*Caron v. R.K.O. Radio Pictures Inc.,* 28 N.Y.S. 2d 1020, aff'd 35 N.Y.S. 2d 715). The Court also dismissed the complaint for defamation of plaintiff's character, adding:

It is the uniqueness of the automobile, together with the television pictures of a black man driving a vehicle and the script dealing with pimps from which plaintiff seeks to draw the inference that he is being so described. Plaintiff, however, neither alleges that he is the person shown driving the vehicle nor that the vehicle driven was the same as the Lincoln Continental shown nor that the emblem on the Lincoln Continental could be or was seen by the viewing audience, nor that his ownership of the vehicle was ever alluded to. There is not the obliquest reference to the plaintiff. Thus the inference which plaintiff seeks to draw is, in the opinion of the court, strained and the cause of action insufficient. Even if the court were not so inclined to dismiss the complaint on that basis, on the face of the complaint itself the qualifiedly privileged nature of the broadcast is apparent and the allegation of malice is insufficient (see *New Times Co. v. Sullivan,* 376 U.S. 254; see also *Gertz v. Robert Welch Inc.,* 418 U.S. 323; *Cera v. Gannett Co., Inc.,* 47 A.D. 2d 797; see *Commercial Programming Unlimited v Columbia Broadcasting System, Inc.,* 81 Misc. 2d 678).

Mistaken Identity May Be Libel

Suppose a newspaper published a story about Mr. John Jones, who has been accused of committing a crime. There is more than one John Jones in the city, however, and the newspaper published a picture of the wrong Mr. Jones with its story. The result is libel. Similarly, in a case where a testimonial for a particular brand of whiskey was signed by one person and the publication used a picture of the wrong person with it, the court held that the plaintiff's grievance should be submitted to a jury.[9]

Pictures of a Place

Improper use of a photograph to illustrate a story can even extend to pictures of buildings. Where, for example, an article on illegal banking procedures was dressed up with the photograph of an innocent banking institution, the bank won a jury verdict for libel.[10]

Retouching Photos

One other area which requires comment involves retouching of photographs. Although this problem has already been covered in the section on model releases in Chapter 2, it is worth noting again that a changed photograph may be objectionable to the subject even though the original was not.

Publication of Wrong Photograph

A New York Civil Court judge has ruled that a former public official whose picture is erroneously published in a newspaper must prove only gross negligence not actual malice (*Beck v. N.Y. Times,* Civil Court, New York).[11] Denying a motion for summary judgment, the court ordered a trial to determine whether the newspaper, *The New York Times,* had been grossly negligent.

The suit arose from a news story published in the *Times* on Dec. 22, 1973, headlined "Beck Acquitted in Security Sales." The article concerned one Louis Beck, a lawyer and former treasurer of the State Democratic Party. An accompanying photograph was in fact one of a Louis Beck, but not the Beck in the story. Instead it showed a former confidential assistant to New York County Surrogate, Samuel DiFalco. The *Times* acknowledged the error in a correction published on Dec. 25, 1973. Mr. Beck, the former aide, subsequently brought the libel action.

In its motion for summary judgment, the *Times* relied on several Supreme Court cases—principally the Sullivan case—which indicated that a public figure must prove actual malice to recover for libel. The paper contended that Mr. Beck, the plaintiff, was a public figure because (1) he had previously been covered by the *Times* for a bribe conspiracy charge to which he pleaded guilty, and (2) the December 22nd article was a matter of public interest.

Without directly deciding whether Mr. Beck was a public or private figure, the judge said the action was governed by *Chapadeau v. Utica Observer-Dispatch Inc.,* handed down by the Court of Appeals late in 1975. That decision, the judge acknowledged, was handed down after the parties in the Beck suit had filed papers.

In *Chapadeau,* which involved a teacher arrested on drug charges, "the Court of Appeals was confronted with the standard of fault to be applied in our state where plaintiff is a private individual and the communication one of a general interest," the civil court judge said.

After analyzing the *Chapadeau* ruling, the judge concluded that "gross negligence is thus the newly-devised standard of fault now to be applied in our courts." The judge ordered a trial to determine "whether defendant's conduct was sufficient to comply with industry standards or was so insufficient as to come within the realm of being grossly negligent."

Within a month following the Beck decision the U.S. Supreme Court handed down an important decision answering the question as to when a seemingly public figure is not a public figure for the purpose of determining the standard of evidence required in a libel case against a publication. The Supreme Court ruled that a Florida socialite who was often mentioned in society reports in the press, whose divorce proceedings were widely reported, and who herself gave news conferences during those proceedings, could not be considered a "public figure" for the purpose of deciding libel claims arising from her divorce proceedings.

The Court issued this ruling in deciding an appeal brought by Time Inc. from a $100,000 libel award won by the woman, Mary Alice Firestone, on the basis of Time's alleged misreporting of the divorce decree entered at her husband's request at the close of the divorce proceedings. The Court reasoned that Mrs. Firestone had no major role "in the affairs of society" and that she had not willingly thrust herself "to the forefront" of a public controversy in an effort to influence its outcome.

The importance of this decision is that if Mrs. Firestone was a "public figure" she would have to prove "actual malice" against Time Inc. in order to succeed in her libel suit. However, if she was not a "public figure" she would just have to prove "fault" on the part of the publication (*Time Inc. v. Firestone,* U.S. Supreme Court, decided March 2, 1976, 96 Sup. Ct. 958). It should be noted that the Supreme Court merely required proof of "fault" on the part of the publication rather than "gross negligence" as did the Beck case. The Supreme Court's decision must therefore be regarded as expressing the present state of the law on the right of an individual who is not a public figure to sue a publication for libel arising from the wrongful or improper use of a photograph or the content of an article or news story.

Conclusion

Finally, let it be noted once again that most cases arising under the law of libel involve questions of fact for the jury to decide. It is wise, therefore, for the photographer to examine carefully those pictures which are intended for publication, particularly the captions, if known, and to avoid those which might seem clever but could possibly hold the subject up to ridicule. In view of the cases involving publication of the wrong photograph, it is also well to verify the identity of the subject of the photograph where it is to be used in connection with an article or news story concerning a particular individual.

CHAPTER VIII

Photographs As Evidence

At the outset it should be noted that many books on the subject of evidence have been written. In these the subject of photographs as evidence has been treated in far greater detail than it is possible to do in the space allocated for this subject in this book. What follows is a brief discussion of the subject designed to give photographers a general idea of the use of photographs in a courtroom. However, in the latter part of this Chapter, references to other books and writings on the subject, with excerpts, are included.

In general, photographs, when shown to be a correct resemblance of the person or thing represented, are competent as evidence. The highest court in New York[1] has commented as follows on photographs as evidence:

> We do not fail to notice, and we may notice judicially, that all civilized communities rely upon photographic pictures for taking and presenting resemblances of persons and animals, of scenery and all natural objects, of buildings and other artificial objects. It is of frequent occurrence, that fugitives from justice are arrested on the identification given by them. "The Rogues' Gallery" is the practical judgment of the executive officers of the law on their efficiency and accuracy. They are signs of the things taken.
>
> A portrait or a miniature taken by a skilled artist, and proven to be an accurate likeness, would be received on a question of the identity or the appearance of a person not producible in court. Photographic pictures do not differ in kind of proof from the pictures of a painter. They are the products of natural laws and a scientific process. It is true that in the hands of a bungler, who is not apt in the use of the process, the result may not be satisfactory. Somewhat [sic] depends for exact likeness upon the nice adjustment of machinery, upon atmospheric conditions, upon the position of the subject, the intensity of the light, the length of the sitting. It is the skill of the operator that takes care of these, as it is the skill of the artist that makes correct drawing of features, and nice mingling of tints, for the portrait. Most of evidence is but the signs of things. . . .
>
> So the signs of the portrait and the photograph, if authenticated by other testimony, may give truthful representations. When shown by such testimony to be correct resemblances of a person, we see not why they may not be shown to the triers of the facts, not as conclusive, but as aids in determining the matter in issue, still being open like proofs of identity or similar matter, to rebuttal or doubt.

Physical Appearance and Identity

In actions for personal injuries courts have permitted photographic evidence as to the appearance of persons. In one case a photograph of the injured person showing the manner in which his limbs had been contracted was admitted into evidence after a physician certified that it was taken in his presence and correctly represented the condition of his limbs. It should, of course, be pointed out that a proper foundation must first be laid for the introduction of the photograph, consisting of testimony that the picture is a true representation of the condition of the person as of a particular time. The court in this case said:

> During the trial, the plaintiff's counsel offered in evidence a photograph of the plaintiff showing the manner in which his limbs were contracted. This was permitted by the court under the objection of the defendant. Before it was done, however, one of the doctors testified that the photograph was taken in his presence and that it correctly represented the condition of the limbs. The only materiality of this evidence was to show the manner in which the limbs of the plaintiff were contracted. In this regard, the testimony of the physician is that it was a correct representation of them. This made it competent as a map or diagram.[2]

Of course, there are very definite limitations on the use of photographs as evidence. If it can be shown that the photograph does not represent the true condition of the subject of the case or that it is misleading, it will not be received in evidence. For example, where the issue in the case was the appearance of a young girl at the time of an accident, a photograph taken one year before the accident was held on appeal to have been improperly received in evidence. The Appellate Court said:

> A photograph of the plaintiff, taken a year before the employment, in the dress worn by her when she received her first Holy Communion, was admitted in evidence over the defendant's objection, upon testimony to the effect that it correctly represented the plaintiff's appearance at the time of the accident; that she was about the size indicated by the photograph when employed; and that the picture looked as she did when she was employed. We all know that dress alone makes a great deal of difference in the apparent age of a person. The combination of dress and a photograph would be doubly deceptive. When employed, the plaintiff was six months below the age fixed by the statute. A photograph taken a year before, dressed as she was, with veil and flowers on her head, short white dress, white slippers and stockings, was no evidence of her appearance as to age when employed. The prejudicial character of the photograph is manifest. It could have served no possible purpose except to mislead, and its misleading character is the more manifest when we consider that the question at issue was the apparent age of a girl at a rapidly developing period of her life.[3]

In an action for death caused by negligence, the admission of a photo of the defendant and his children taken about six months before his death was also held[4] erroneous as calculated to arouse the sympathy of the jury. And in an action for personal injuries to a vaudeville dancer who was struck by an automobile, an Appellate Court reversed a decision of the Trial Court to permit the introduction of a motion picture on the following grounds: the film, showing the plaintiff dancing *prior* to the accident despite an artificial leg (which did not prevent him from carrying on his work) was inadmissible since it made a farce of the trial. The Court said:

> Aside from the fact that moving pictures present a fertile field for exaggeration of any emotion or action, and the absence of evidence as to how this particular motion picture was prepared, we think the picture admitted in evidence brought before the jury irrelevant matter, hearsay and incompetent evidence and tended to make a farce of the trial.[5]

In another case it was held that in actions for personal injuries capable of verbal description, it was error to admit a photograph of the injuries into evidence.[6]

Thus it can be seen from the foregoing that pictures are admissible only under certain conditions and where a proper foundation for them has first been laid.

Condition of Premises

The rules governing admission of photos to show the physical condition and identity of persons apply to photographs depicting the condition of premises. Thus it has been held[7] that in an action for damages to premises, a photograph of the premises at the time of the accident is admissible. And in another case, a high court in New York stated the rule:

> If a fair representation of the premises, it was admissible as an aid in the investigation, as much so as a map or other diagram and served in a like manner to explain or illustrate and apply testimony. . . . Of course, its value, like the value of other evidence, depends upon its accuracy.

Moving Pictures

There have been numerous cases involving the propriety of the admission of moving pictures in evidence. A court[8] held that if the pictures are sensational only and unnecessary, particularly where the facts may be described or evidence submitted in another form, they should be excluded. The court said:

The admissibility in evidence of moving pictures has been before the courts of the state several times and there appears to be very decided and divergent views with reference to their admission in evidence. . . . In no case should they be admitted unless a proper foundation has been laid therefor. In most cases the question should be left largely to the discretion of the trial judge. If a trial is to be unduly delayed by exhibiting moving pictures, the court may very properly refuse to permit such a delay. If moving pictures are sensational only and unnecessary, the court should refuse to permit such evidence, particularly where the facts may be described or the evidence submitted in another form and thus avoid the delay and difficulty which will result from their introduction. If their use is solely for the purpose of advertisement or in an effort to obtain publicity, they should not be allowed in evidence. Several cases have been cited where evidence of moving pictures has been properly rejected. In these cases the purpose was shown to be merely sensational. Where there is no need of such pictures, as in several of the cases adverted to, the trial court is within its right in rejecting such testimony.

References on the Subject of Evidence

References to books and writings on the subject of evidence as well as brief excerpts in which the role of photographs is discussed are included in the following section. However, the books themselves should be consulted for a more detailed consideration of the subject matter.

In "Planning and Trying Cases" by Charles W. Fricke, Judge of the Superior Court, Los Angeles County, the following excellent statement is made in introducing the subject of "Photographs and Photographic Evidence":

Photographs, as evidence, may be divided into those which have an illustrative value and those which of themselves have probative force. Those which are purely illustrative, picturing the scene of a crime, the intersection where a collision occurred or some physical object, will help greatly in enabling the jurors to understand and visualize the matters covered by the testimony of the witnesses. The value of such photographs lies in the fact that with their assistance the jury will better know what a place or object looked like than they could from any amount of verbal description from the witness stand. Then, also, there is the psychological factor that a case, thus illustrated, is more interesting to the jurors. Jurors like to see photographs and physical objects relevant to the case and will pay closer attention because of the enlistment of their interest.

The illustrative photograph allows the jurors to visualize what occurred and to view and evaluate the testimony of the witnesses very much as if the testimony were being given before the jury at the place shown by the picture. To give the jurors this opportunity of knowing what the place they are hearing about looks like and receiving the full value of the testimony, such photographs should be introduced into evidence and shown to the jury at the earliest possible stage of the trial, as the value of the photograph is largely lost if not seen by the jury until after testimony which the photograph would illustrate has been given.

Where the picture is relevant and not objectionable per se there is little difficulty in getting it into evidence; all that is required is the testimony of a witness that the photograph is a fair representation of a particular subject. The law does not require the testimony of the person who took the picture nor that of the person who did the developing and finishing as a requisite to admissibility.

Where more than one photograph of the same subject has been taken to show the appearance from different viewpoints or distances or because one picture can not cover the entire subject, such photographs should be treated as a set and the entire set introduced and shown to the jury. While the practise of making marks on photographic exhibits, to indicate particular points or objects, should be used sparingly, it is of value at times, but when such markings are made they should as in the case of marking maps and diagrams be distinctive. Although it can only be done by the consent of the parties, it will prove of great assistance to everybody concerned if there be endorsed on the back of each photograph the general nature of the subject portrayed and such further notation, such as "looking North," as counsel may agree.

Although poor technical quality or poor technique will not of itself render a photograph inadmissible, there is little excuse for the poor quality of the photographs often seen in court. Aside from the fact that a good photograph is better to look at, the value of a photograph as evidence depends largely and is directly proportionate to the quality of the photograph as such and the skill of the photographer in selecting the proper point and angle of view and the conditions under which the picture is taken.

In "Law Enforcement and Police Photography" (*Encyclopedia of Photography,* page 1973) the following statement appears in the introduction to the subject:

Law Enforcement and Photography have become inseparable allies in the war on crime and violence. Pictures frequently reveal the events that led up to a crime, accident, or fire. They help establish facts and provide a permanent record which can prove invaluable to investigators, attorneys, judges, witnesses, juries, and defendants. Often a good picture means the difference between conviction and acquittal.

Indicative of the value of photography in law enforcement is the fact that police departments in smaller towns and communities are following the example of the larger cities by arming their officers with cameras. That the modern police department considers photography more than just a medium to record evidence to convict criminals is demonstrated by the wide variety of uses of police pictures. Many departments use still and motion pictures to train personnel, make traffic studies, and further public relations in their communities.

One of the newest applications of police photography is to record on motion-picture film arrests in which the suspect offers resistance. The practice has been instituted by at least one metropolitan law enforcement agency to counter charges of police brutality.

In general there are three primary ways of using photography in law enforcement: (1) as a means of identifying an individual through a photograph made at some previous time; (2) as a method of discovering, recording, or preserving evidence relating to an accident or crime; and (3) in the courtroom, as a way of presenting to the jurors an impression of the pertinent elements of a crime.

In *McCormick on Evidence,* the following statement is made by the author, regarding the use of photographs as evidence:

As with demonstrative evidence generally, the prime condition on admissibility is that the photograph be identified by a witness as a portrayal of certain facts relevant to the issue, and verified by such a witness on personal knowledge as a correct representation of these facts. The witness who thus lays the foundation need not be the photographer nor need the witness know anything of the time or conditions of the taking. It is the facts represented, the scene or the object, that he must know about, and when this knowledge is shown, he can say whether the photograph correctly portrays these facts. When the photograph is thus verified it comes in as demonstrative evidence which is part of the testimony of the witness, and incorporated in it by reference. The adjective "illustrative" aptly describes the role of the picture thus incorporated in the testimony, but it is sometimes used as contrasted with "substantive" evidence. It is believed that this distinction is groundless, and that the photograph, as part of the descriptive testimony, is just as much substantive evidence as the testimony of a witness describing the features of a scene or object without a photograph would be. It may be correctly described as both "illustrative" and "substantive."

The interest and vividness of photographs may be heightened by the creative ingenuity of counsel in planning for the photographing of posed, or artificially reconstructed scenes. People, automobiles, and other objects are placed on the scene to conform to the descriptions of the original crime or collision given by the witnesses. When the posed photographs go no further than to portray the positions of the persons and objects as reflected in the undisputed testimony, their admission is generally approved. When the photographs portray the reconstructed scene as testified to by the proponent's witnesses, but the adversary's testimony is or will be substantially conflicting as to the features and positions pictured, then there is danger that one party's version will be unduly emphasized, and the judge should have a discretion to exclude the posed photograph, unless opportunity can be afforded to the opponent to prepare a similar pictured reconstruction of the scene as portrayed by his witnesses.

With respect to the admission of moving pictures, with or without sound, the element of discretion is more often emphasized in the opinions, than in cases involving still pictures. Perhaps the principal reason for this is administrative. While the principles applied to still pictures are generally applicable here the still picture entails only a minimum expenditure of time and little distraction of attention. But to show the movie in court, a good deal of time must be spent in installing the projector and screen, darkening and arranging the courtroom, and in the showing of the film, and may involve likewise a good deal of diversion of attention from the issues and interruption of the march of the trial. Moreover, there are great possibilities of distortion and falsification due to the choice of light, angle, speed and position of the camera, but these are different in degree only from the possibilities of perversion of still pictures.

These considerations loomed as larger obstacles to the judges when this kind of evidence was first offered than they do today when the use of them in court has lost the shock of novelty. Undoubtedly the discretion has always been more favorably exercised in the admission of moving-pictures of what we have called the original (non-posed) sort, such as pictures of personal injury claimants climbing trees or playing baseball, than in the case of pictures of artificial or reconstructed activities. Even these latter have recently been allowed to be shown when their value seemed to outweigh their danger. Although it is desirable to have the operator present to testify to the fact that the machine was operated normally as to lighting, speed, angle and position, it may be sufficient, unless the judge in his discretion requires further verification, for any person who witnessed the scene pictured to testify that the picture faithfully represented the objects and activities as he saw them. Undoubtedly this process of reproducing movement, background, color and sound will more and more be recognized by lawyers and judges as a valuable resource for adding vividness, accuracy and entertainment to the presentation of facts.

CHAPTER IX

Photography—
Business, Art or Profession?

Business, art or profession—what is photography? And what difference does it make? The question can arise in various ways and is one of particular importance legally to the professional photographer. Here is why.

A photographer opens a studio in a community which has an unincorporated business tax. The law exempts persons engaged in a profession. Is the photographer exempt? A license tax is imposed on those engaged in a mechanical pursuit. Is the photographer included? A law exempts implements of trade from levy by creditors. Is a lens an implement of trade? Regulations are imposed on manufacturing businesses. Do they apply to a particular photographic business? These are but a few of the many instances in which the courts have been called upon to define the status of photography.

The courts have called photography everything from a trade to a science. There has been no unanimity of opinion on the subject, but the courts have generally said that the photographer should be regarded as an artist.

Back in 1890 a Louisiana court had to decide whether a photographer should pay a certain tax. The state constitution exempted all persons engaged in mechanical pursuits from the payment of the tax, and the photographer claimed the exemption. In denying the exemption, the court said that, as distinguished from a mechanical pursuit, photography is a science, or at least a liberal art, in which the desired results could not be accomplished by the spontaneous action of the apparatus employed, but required the agency of a photographer

> who, to operate successfully, must necessarily be, and prove himself, a most intelligent artist, calling into activity not only his hands, senses and body, but also and chiefly, in order to control them, his scientific aptitudes and superintending mind. . . . The science or art which he practices is not a useful or mechanical science or art (one in which the hands and body are more concerned than the brain), but at least, a liberal or polite art— scientific to a quite considerable extent, the practice of which is made efficient and valuable only by knowledge and skill, as the result of some science, observation, combination and experimentation not readily acquired.[1]

A Tennessee court took a similar view in 1883, when it ruled that a photographer is not a mechanic within the meaning of a statute which exempted mechanics' tools from seizure to satisfy a judgment. The Court said:

> The photographer is an artist, not an artisan, who takes impressions or likenesses of things and persons on prepared plates or surfaces. He is no more a mechanic than the painter who, by means of his pigments, covers his canvas with the glaring images of natural objects.[2]

Over thirty years ago a British court decided that a photographer is not a professional man. The photographer offered proof to show that his photographs were different from those of the average photographer. The court recognized him as an outstanding photographer but refused to elevate him to the status of a professional man, saying:

> It was true that the appellant's work differed from that of an ordinary photographer. He had gone very much beyond the work of the ordinary trade photographer, but he did not, as it appeared to him [his Lordship] do anything in law beyond what an ordinary photographer did.[3]

Of course, the decision of the British court assumes that there can be no question that an ordinary photographer is not a professional man, and the argument advanced for the photographer in question was that he was an extraordinary photographer. Any distinction between ordinary and extraordinary photographers seems baseless, for if photography itself is a profession, anyone practicing it is a professional man.

The New York courts have not found it necessary to classify photography specifically, but a New York court did say in 1931 that a photographic business could not be classified as manufacturing.[4]

A business tax is imposed in New York on unincorporated business. Persons engaged in a profession are exempt. Photographers have not yet tested whether this law applies to them, but if they should, here is the test of a profession, established by the highest court in the state, which they will have to meet. A profession requires "knowledge of an advanced type in a given field of science or learning gained by a prolonged course of specialized instruction and study."[5]

Licensing Statutes

Further clues as to the status of photography in the eyes of the law are found in decisions involving the right of states to require licenses from those desiring to engage in photography. In most states where such legislation was enacted the courts have invalidated the statutes as being unwarranted interference with the right of an individual to engage in a lawful occupation which does not so affect the public welfare as to warrant state regulation. An Arizona Court in 1941 held:

The *business or profession* of taking photographs of people, animals and things does not need regulation. It is one of the innocent, usual occupations in which everybody who wishes may indulge as a pastime or a hobby or a vocation, without harm or injury to anybody, or to the general welfare, or the public health and morals, or the peace, safety and comfort of the people. It needs no policing.[6]

In 1935 a photographer was convicted in a Hawaiian Court of practicing without a license. The conviction was over-ruled on appeal. The Appellate Court said:

More specifically the question is, was it within the constitutional power of the legislature to exclude from the practice of photography for profit all persons who had not complied with the provisions of the Act? The answer to this inquiry depends on the nature of photography—whether as an occupation it is innocent and innocuous or whether it is infected with some quality that might render it dangerous to the morals, the health, the comfort or welfare of those who constitute the public. If the latter is true it is within the police power of the legislature to place upon it the regulations and restrictions contained in the Act. If, on the other hand, the practice of photography is harmless and without detriment to the public welfare, it was beyond the power of the legislature to restrict it to those having a certificate of proficiency.[7]

The Court concluded that the act requiring a license for the practice of photography "is an unconstitutional encroachment upon the liberty of the citizen to choose and pursue an innocent occupation."

In 1938 a Tennessee Court, in over-ruling similar legislation said:

We find it difficult to perceive just how the licensing of photographers and regulation of the taking and finishing of pictures . . . has any real tendency to protect the public health or the public morals.[8]

A Georgia court struck down similar legislation,[9] and in 1955 the Montana Supreme Court struck down the Photographic Examiners Act which required persons desiring to engage in portrait, commercial work or photo finishing to procure a license. The Act provided that those engaged in the practice of photography, when it took effect, should be granted a license upon application, but that others must given satisfactory evidence as to competency and fitness to practice photography based on technical knowledge and business integrity. The Court said that the only basis for the Act was to create a monopoly for those persons fortunate enough to be included within the formula of the Act prior to the date it became effective and that the Act was not in the interest of the general welfare. It also condemned the law on the ground that it gave the examining board unlimited authority to choose who was qualified as a photographer. Also in 1955, the Nevada State Assembly refused to act on a proposed law for licensing photographers.

The only discordant judicial note on the licensing question appears to have been sounded in a decision of the North Carolina Courts. It was there decided, by a three-to-two decision, that a photography licensing act was constitutional. However, the dissenting judge in that case said:

> I am therefore unable to conceive how the practice of photography has such a rational and substantial relationship to social needs or to public health, safety and good morals as to make it a subject of legislation under the police power of the state. . . . The regulation of business and professions, through administrative licensing, has heretofore been limited to those professions having a direct and positive relation to the health, safety or morals of the community. The trade of photography bears no general resemblance to any of the professions indicated. . . . While photography requires some skill, it is the same type of skill required by other trades and vocations.[10]

While this statement is in a dissenting opinion and does not represent the view of the majority of the North Carolina court, it seems to be the view of the great majority of the courts in the United States. In other words, the courts have generally freed photography from the shackles of the police power of the states, but at the same time have refused to elevate it to the legal status of a profession.

Photography has made important progress since some of the cases referred to were decided. A vocational guidance pamphlet issued by the Rochester Institute of Technology in 1950 indicates how specialized photography as we know it today has become. There it is noted that many branches exist in the field, such as advertising photography, aerial photography, commercial photography, documentary photography, industrial and scientific photography, motion picture photography, museum photography and photo journalism. Furthermore, a number of colleges and universities have seen fit to accord to photography the status of an art or science by giving courses leading to degrees with majors in photography.* However, these are not legally required courses as a prerequisite to engaging in the practice of photography and anyone is permitted to earn his living at photography in most states. As long as this situation exists, photography cannot meet the legal test of a profession as laid down by the New York courts, namely, requiring knowledge of an advanced type in a given field of science or learning gained by a prolonged course of specialized instruction and study.

However, photography has not fared too badly in the courts. The weight of authority is in favor of regarding a photographer as an artist. The

---

*Rochester Institute of Technology (Assoc. in Applied Science); Ohio University (Bachelor of Fine Arts. Major in Photography); University of Houston (Bachelor of Arts, Science or Fine Arts. Major in Photography); University of Southern California (Bachelor of Arts. Major in Cinema); Santa Monica City College (Associate in Applied Science); Institute of Design, Illinois Institute of Technology (Bachelor of Science in Photography); Maryland State College (Bachelor of Science in Industrial Education or in Mechanical Arts. Major in Photography); Oklahoma Baptist University (Bachelor of Science. Major in Photography).

courts have almost uniformly come to the rescue of photography whenever state regulatory control has been attempted and, except for a few states, licenses are not required in order to engage in professional photography. The courts have stamped photography as an innocent occupation or vocation which may be engaged in without harm or injury to anybody or to the general welfare. The inability of the courts to find a few magic words that will pin a definite label on photography has obviously not prevented this sometime hobby-business-art-profession from flourishing over the years.

More important than the label is the vast area of the rights and obligations of the photographer, both amateur and professional. Right of privacy, restrictions on the taking of photographs, libel, ownership of photographs, copyrights—these and still other areas of law affect everyone who snaps a shutter.

Licensing Requirements for Photographers in 50 States*

State	No Licensing Provision	Licensing for Fee Only
Alabama		X (a)
Alaska		X (l)
Arizona	X (b)	
Arkansas		X (f)
California	X	
Colorado	X	
Connecticut	X	
Delaware		X (a)
Florida		X (d)
Georgia	X (e)	
Hawaii	X	
Idaho	X (j)	
Illinois	X	
Indiana	X	
Iowa	X	
Kansas	X	
Kentucky	X	
Louisiana		X
Maine		X (c)
Maryland	X (k)	
Massachusetts	X	
Michigan	X	
Minnesota	X	
Mississippi	X	
Missouri	X (f)	
Montana	X	
Nebraska	X	
Nevada	X	
New Hampshire		X (c)
New Jersey	X (f)	

State	License Required	No State License
New Mexico		X
New York	X	
North Carolina		X (l)
North Dakota	X	
Ohio	X (g)	
Oklahoma	X (f)	
Oregon	X (f)	
Pennsylvania	X (f)	
Rhode Island	X	
South Carolina	X (f)	
South Dakota	X	
Tennessee	X (h)	
Texas	X	
Utah	X (f)	
Vermont		X (c)
Virginia		X (f)(i)
Washington	X (h)	
West Virginia	X (l)	
Wisconsin	X	
Wyoming	X (g)	

*In 1976 a review was made of the licensing provisions of each of the 50 states. In most cases the information set forth concerning licensing requirements was derived from the text of individual statutes. In others, the authors have relied upon communications from the Secretary of State.

Notes on chart of Licensing Statutes:

(a) Statute so worded as to apply to professional photographers only.

(b) Act of 1935 was declared unconstitutional by the Arizona Supreme Court.

(c) Applies only to itinerant photographers.

(d) License must be obtained from Tax Collector of County where photographer does business.

(e) 1937 Statute set up a State Board of Photographic Examiners but was declared unconstitutional. *Bramley v. State,* (1939) 187 Ga. 826, 2 S.E. (2nd) 647.

(f) Although no State License is required, Statutes provide that cities, or some classes of cities, shall have the power to pass ordinances requiring license for regulation or revenue and inquiry should be made with local authorities.

(g) Bill introduced in 1940 failed to pass.

(h) Although no license is required, photographers, except newspaper photographers, are specificially taxed for doing business.

(i) Virginia also has Statute regulating practice of photography. See act of 1938, 544.

(j) Although no license is required, photographers who sell merchandise, such as picture frames, must obtain a store license.

(k) Although no State license is required, Baltimore City requires a license for persons engaged in the business of taking photographs on the streets or sidewalks.

(l) Annual privilege license is required from State Department of Revenue.

CHAPTER X

Questions and Answers

Further details on many of the points of law considered in the previous chapters are explained in the answers to the questions that follow. These questions are typical of the ones addressed to us as columnists for *Popular Photography* magazine and cover the subjects which most frequently concern the amateur photographer in particular.

Question. Can pictures of accidents on a state thruway be taken without obtaining a special permit?

Answer. Pictures may be taken on a state thruway or any other highway whether it is a toll road or not. No permit is necessary.

Question. Can I take pictures in "public" places? Can the management of a railroad station, library, department store or theatre prevent a camera from being brought in or being used for the purpose of taking candid pictures of the crowds?

Answer. Pictures can generally be taken in public places. However, libraries, museums, theatres, etc., do have the right to prohibit cameras from being used on the premises or to make whatever restrictions they wish to impose on the taking of pictures. Note that the right to take a picture is not the same as the right to use it, however. Persons who have their pictures taken in public or elsewhere may have a claim for invasion of privacy if the use made of the picture can be classified as advertising for trade purposes.

Question. I plan to go to Europe this year and will want to photograph as much color as possible. In snapping candids of people in their own surroundings the element of spontaneity is often lost when the subject is approached to ask permission to photograph them before taking the picture. Is it advisable to take a candid photo without the subject's permission?

Answer. It can generally be said that it is not necessary to obtain someone's consent just to take his picture. You must remember that the reason for getting a release or written consent is to permit you to use or publish the picture for advertising or trade purposes. As long as the use which you make of a photograph taken gratuitously is not for advertising or trade purposes and is not libelous in nature, you will generally have no problem.

Question. I plan to take a trip to Mexico and intend to take moving pictures there. Are there any restrictions?

Answer. Yes. Much of the literature distributed by the Mexican Tourist Department and many travel directories indicate that filming with movie cameras other than 8mm or super 8mm is not allowed for persons using a tourist card in Mexico. Such literature informs those who intend to use commercial equipment (16mm) that permits are necessary and indicates where to apply for them.

Question. I would like to take pictures of photographs which I have seen in your magazine. Do I have to ask for permission from the publisher?

Answer. Under our copyright laws it would be incumbent upon you, before copying any pictures from magazines or other sources, to find out whether they are copyrighted, for the copyright owner of a picture is the only one who has the right to reproduce it. If the magazine carries a copyright notice, you should obtain permission of the copyright owner before making copies. If you are just making the copies for your own amusement or for educational purposes, there is usually no difficulty in obtaining the necessary consent.

Question. Is it necessary for me to have a model release to sell a picture of a car, truck or farm machinery to a magazine or company for illustrations or advertising?

Answer. It is generally believed that you may sell photographs (which you own) of automobiles or farm machinery without obtaining a release from the owner of the particular piece of equipment since the right of privacy protects persons, but not property. The authors know of several lawsuits, however, where the owner of a home or other property claimed that property rights were violated when a photographer took a picture of the home and sold it for an advertising illustration, but these cases were settled before trial. The authors do not know of any case which has decided this question one way or the other, though there have been cases involving photos of property where a decision was based on who owned the photograph and on whether a libel had been committed on the owner of the property. A picture of a reputable bank accompanying an article on crooked banking, for example, was held to be a libel on the bank.

Question. I am an amateur photographer and have talked to one of my friends who is a surgeon about taking a picture of an operation he will perform in the hospital. Will I need a release to publish the picture?

Answer. There have been many court decisions in which the use of a photograph of a person undergoing medical treatment was held to be an invasion of the right of privacy. Technically, the use of such pictures to illustrate articles on medicine should not constitute an invasion of privacy when the use of the picture does not violate one's sense of decency, and some courts have so ruled. Since people are more likely to be sensitive about such pictures it is really important to get consent, and the consent should be both broad and specific. It is also clear that the consent of a patient to medical or surgical treatment is not tantamount to a consent to take pictures of him in treatment.

Question. I took a picture of a motel for a booklet put out by a local club. A few months later an advertising salesman for the local newspaper asked me for a print of this picture. I quoted him a price for it and he replied, "Why should I pay for a reprint? I will just cut the photograph out of the booklet and make another picture." Does he have a right to do this?

Answer. If the picture that you took was properly copyrighted, no one can reproduce your picture without violating the copyright laws. Someone could, however, take another picture of the same motel and use it without violating the copyright law.

Question. I plan to sell some of my photographs to magazines as well as enter them in national contests. Some examples of these pictures are a full bench of people in Rockefeller Center Plaza; a picture of an Amish man in a Pennsylvania market; people lining the rail of a Manhattan sight-seeing ferryboat; an old sea captain on the New England coast. The people in the pictures did not know I was photographing them at the time and I did not ask them for releases. Can my pictures be published even though I do not have the releases?

Answer. Model releases are generally required in cases where pictures are to be used for purposes of advertising or trade. If a picture is published by a photographic magazine as a contest winner or for other editorial purposes, and if the pictures do not hold a person up to ridicule or are not otherwise offensive, it is the opinion of the authors that consent of the subject should not be necessary. It is still best, of course, to have the consent.

Question. I took pictures of an accident and would like to know whether, if I sell them to some interested party or an insurance company, I have the right to sell the same pictures to anyone else.

Answer. Assuming that you are a free-lance photographer and not in the employ of any publication, when you take pictures of the accident, you have the absolute right to dispose of them under whatever terms or conditions you desire. When you wish to sell such pictures you have the option to sell either all rights to the picture, or one-time reproduction rights only, or you might make a different arrangement. Before the selling of the prints you should be sure to affix a notice of copyright on the prints, for in the situation you describe, you would not get the protection a photographer normally gets when he sells pictures to a publication. In the latter case he is protected by the copyright notice the publisher places in the magazine. Thus, if you protect yourself by appropriate copyright notice and by appropriate contract arrangement, you would have the right to sell as many prints as you may wish. On the other hand, if you sell all rights to the picture, then you would have no right to resell the prints.

Question. I am a professional portrait photographer of children. Do I need a release from the parents in order to enter a photograph of their child in a contest sponsored by a photographic magazine?

Answer. When you are engaged to take pictures for a fee, the relationship between you and your customer is such that while you may retain the physical possession of the negatives, you cannot do anything with them without the consent of the customer. New York and some other states would permit you to exhibit the picture on the premises of your photographic studio as samples of your work, but if the customer objects, you would have to remove the picture. Thus, the consent of the customer must be obtained before entering his picture in a contest, and the child being a minor, you would have to obtain the consent of a parent. The situation would be different in some respects if you had taken the pictures gratuitously or if they happened to be candid shots.

Question. If I take a picture of a store or other private property with the consent of the owner to use it in an ad, and then I sell the picture for that purpose, is the owner of the store or other private property which was photographed entitled to any part of the profit from the sale of the photograph?

Answer. Since you have permission of the owner of the property and the owner has made no agreement with you regarding the division of the profit from the sale of the picture, you would not be legally obligated to give him any part of the profit. Having given his consent, the question is purely one of contract and since the owner did not protect himself he would have no claim against you.

Question. I took photographs at a local summer resort for advertising purposes but did not obtain releases from the persons in the photographs. They were guests in the hotel. The owners of the resort want to use the pictures and are willing to assume full responsibility. If anyone sues me, will I be covered by such an agreement?

Answer. This agreement would protect you providing the resort owner is financially sound. (In several states the agreement must be made in writing.) You must remember that you will continue to be liable to the people shown in the pictures. The resort owner, by assuming responsibility, agrees to reimburse you for any damages awarded against you, but if at that time the resort is out of business or otherwise insolvent, then the agreement to indemnify you, while legally good, would naturally be a worthless piece of paper.

Question. I am starting out as a candid wedding photographer. If the pictures I take at a wedding do not turn out well, can I be sued by the people who engaged me to take the pictures?

Answer. If you hold yourself out to be a professional photographer, competent to take pictures of a wedding and you fall down on the job, then you can be sued and held liable unless you can show you were not at fault. When you hold yourself out as a professional, the law requires that you do a good and workmanlike job. If, on the other hand, you tell your customer that you are an amateur and that you will merely do your best to do a good job, then the situation would be different and, provided the court accepts your version of the arrangement, it would not hold you liable because the pictures did not turn out well.

Question. A few years ago I entered some of my pictures in a photography contest. I did not win a prize, and this year I asked the sponsor of the contest to return my pictures. I was told the prints and negatives had been destroyed six months after the contest closed in accordance with the rules announced for the contest. Why should they have the right to destroy my pictures?

Answer. The sponsor had a perfect right to dispose of the pictures after the period of time specified in the contest rules. The rules set forth the terms and conditions upon which pictures are submitted. You do not have to submit pictures if the rules are not to your liking. In our experience the publishers of photographic magazines always make some provision in their contest rules for the return of pictures if postage is supplied with the entry, but no one could be expected to keep mountains of pictures on hand year after year just because someone might subsequently ask for the return of his pictures. You might be interested to know that the United States Post Office Department has strict rules which must be observed by sponsors of contests who use the mails in connection with the contests.

Question. I recently took some film to a local camera store for processing. Now I am told by the camera store that the processor lost my film. The pictures on the roll of film were taken at my son's birthday party, and though they aren't worth much to anyone else, they mean a lot to me. Can I sue?

Answer. You might sue, but even if you won your case on the ground of negligence, it would hardly be worth the trouble as a practical matter. Your problem is to establish damage, and this would be extremely difficult in your case. Nevertheless, if there were no other complications, you could receive nominal damages in an amount fixed by the judge or jury. However, you probably were given a receipt at the camera store which contained a limitation of liability to the cost of replacement of film. While the law is not too well settled on the effect of such receipts, there is at least one reported case in the lower court in New York holding that such receipt is a barrier to successful prosecution of your claim.

Question. I recently took some pictures of a model who posed in the nude. I did not get a release, but the model told me when I took the pictures that I could sell them to a magazine. The magazine to whom the pictures were sent wants a written release, but the model has moved out of my town and I cannot find her. Is the release necessary?

Answer. The magazine is right to insist on a written release. Although many states do not require the consent of a subject in writing, the publication of a nude study without such consent is fraught with danger. The publisher as well as the photographer may be sued for invasion of privacy or libel, and no one would want to base his defense on an oral consent. In a recent New York case, a model had posed in the nude for a photographer but orally forbade him to have the picture published in any manner so that her face would show. It was established at the trial that the model had posed in the nude previously with the same restriction. The court awarded her $1500 in damages.

Question. In my town a morals squad recently seized from newsstands without a search warrant, copies of magazines that they claimed were obscene. One of the magazines was a monthly photographic publication containing two nude studies. Does the law allow local police to do this?

Answer. The type of seizure described in this question is a flagrant violation of constitutional rights. The Supreme Court of the United States has outlined in decisions over the past 13 years (see Chapter 5) a definition of "obscene" which, while not precise, is now fairly clear. There can be no doubt that under the tests enunciated by the court, the traditional consumer publications in the photographic field are outside the scope of any conceivable definition of obscenity. It has also been made clear, particularly in one United States Supreme Court case (*Quality of Copies of Books v. State of*

Kansas, 378 U.S. 205 [1964]), that a massive seizure of books or magazines before there is an opportunity for a hearing on the question of whether the books are obscene is a violation of constitutional rights (even in a case where it turns out the books *are* obscene). The traditional rule that "prior restraint" of communications is a violation of the First Amendment (seizing books before any hearing would be a prior restraint) has, however, been weakened by recent decisions of the court, which permit seizure under a search warrant issued by a judge who has first seen the material and believes that there is probable cause for prosecution. (*People v. Steinberg,* 304 N.Y.S. 2d 858; *People v. Bercowitz,* 304 N.Y.S. 2d 963; *People v. Hall,* 304 N.Y.S. 2d 379; *Rage Books, Inc. v. Leary,* D.C. 301 F. Supp. 546).

Question. Should a photographer incorporate?

Answer. This is very much a matter of general business law. The photographer is subject to the same laws which affect other business or professional men and may, of course, apply for the same benefits and advantages. The primary benefit of incorporating is generally considered to be the feature of limitation of liability. This means that if the business is unsuccessful and in debt, or otherwise incurs financial obligations, the individual stockholders need have no fear of being held liable for such obligations. Obviously, there is no sense in an amateur photographer incorporating. As to professional photographers, the advisability of incorporating would depend on the facts in each case. For example, one who works out of his home where he keeps his camera and equipment and accepts photographic assignments would appear to have no need to incorporate. On the other hand, where one or more photographers rent a studio or building under a long-term lease, purchase expensive equipment under installment contracts, make other purchases on credit, have a number of employees, and do business on a large scale, it would probably be advisable to incorporate so that none of the individuals will be personally liable for the business debts if things go wrong.

There are, of course, other considerations. The problem of taxes is important and a photographer should consult his accountant or tax attorney as to the income tax rates which are applicable to each. Also, remember that aside from the original cost and legal fees, once you incorporate you must, in most states, file franchise tax returns every year and pay such tax, whether or not you do business.

Whether the benefit of limitation of personal liability outweighs some of the disadvantages will depend on each individual situation and you are urged to consult an attorney as to whether your case calls for incorporation, operating as an individual, or as a partnership.

Question. What kind of insurance should a photographer carry?

Answer. In answering this question we are, of course, excluding any discussion of life, hospital and accident insurance. For these types of insurance the same considerations apply to the photographer and non-photographer.

As a photographer there are certain types of situations which may give rise to liability on your part in which it would be well to protect oneself against by insurance. Of course, many states now make automobile liability insurance compulsory so that if you live in one of those states, such as New York, you cannot operate a car without such insurance. However, accidents also happen in other places. If you operate a studio, you are exposed to liability for accidents on the premises, such as someone tripping over an extension cord, being burned by a light bulb, being cut by an exploding bulb, falling on a defective floor, injury while entering or leaving your premises or in countless other ways. Therefore, if you are exposed to these situations it would be most desirable for you to carry liability insurance. And don't forget that the difference in premium between a $10,000 and $50,000 policy may not be as great as you think. Juries nowadays in accident cases are known to award large amounts. If you don't have sufficient coverage, your insurance company will pay up to the amount of the policy and you will have to pay the rest yourself. Therefore, don't be deluded into a false sense of security just because you have insurance. Make sure it is in a more than sufficient amount. Consult a competent insurance broker relative to your individual needs.

If you are a free-lance photographer who accepts individual assignments, you may have occasion to send your pictures to a distant processor. You may have to use the mail or express. Make sure you consider insuring the film for its proper value. The premium may be inconsequential in relation to the loss you may suffer if the film is lost. Don't be penny wise and pound foolish. Use a carrier who will provide such insurance.

Suppose you have a stock of valuable pictures which you are trying to sell. Your potential customer, be it an advertising agency, publisher or other, will want you to leave your pictures for consideration. Often the pictures are lost. Insurance to cover such losses should also be considered. Since this insurance is comparatively new the premium may be high. You will have to decide whether or not it pays to carry it. Some picture agencies to whom photographers are constantly sending pictures have an arrangement for such insurance coverage at a small cost to the photographer. You should, of course, insure your equipment against loss as part of your regular personal coverage.

There are other types of insurance peculiar to photography, such as coverage for libel and violation of a person's civil rights by use of the photograph for purposes of trade or advertising without the subject's written consent. While the latter types are sometimes carried by publications, the cost for the individual photographer is likely to be prohibitive.

As the law governing photographers develops further there may be other types of situations making insurance coverage desirable.

We do not advocate that a photographer be covered against "everything." Cost is an important factor, and the decision for or against particular insurance coverage must be made on the basis of the individual situation.

Question. Where a photograph is taken for use as evidence in a law suit, what records should be kept with reference to the picture?

Answer. Before the picture may be used in the trial, there should be preliminary proof of care and accuracy in the taking of the photograph. The photographer should have a complete record of when and where the photo was taken, under what conditions, and be able to discuss the subject of angles, light conditions and distortions.

Question. May a photograph be used in evidence where the subject matter can be brought into court?

Answer. No. Photographs are only copies and the originals must be brought into court. A photograph of a written instrument which can be produced is therefore not admissible. On the other hand, an automobile cannot be brought into court and a photograph may be used in its place.

Question. Are motion pictures showing activities of a person claiming to have been inactivated by an injury admissible in evidence?

Answer. Yes. As a matter of fact, insurance companies have been extremely successful in defeating disability claims based on feigned or exaggerated injuries through the use of motion pictures. Cases are not unusual where the insurance company's photographer follows a claimant for days without the subject's knowledge, taking pictures of the claimant walking, running for trains, climbing steps two at a time, lifting big objects, and other shots likely to be most embarrassing to the unsuspecting claimant at the time of the trial.

Question. How can my camera be an aid to help me recover for property losses resulting from fire, flood, theft, tornado or other disaster where proof of prior ownership and identification of property is necessary?

Answer. Sometime ago, the *New York Times* published an excellent article in its Camera Section on "Taking a Photo Inventory." The article first suggests taking pictures of the outside of the house including shots of all valuable property on the grounds and in the garage (car, boat, motorcycle, gardening equipment, lawn mower, snow removal equipment, etc.). Then proceed to the inside of the house. Take an overall view of each room; then start photographing specific items of value (paintings, antiques, sculpture, television and stereo sets, piano, desks, valuable pieces of furniture, sets of silverware and china, articles of jewelry, typewriters, cameras and accessories, vases, heirlooms, etc.). Contents of desks, closets and drawers should be photographed. Book, stamp and coin collections should also be included in pictures.

After the pictures are processed, prepare a list of each item including the date of picture and price. As to items of clothing, include a numerical count.

Last, but not least, don't leave the pictures and list in the same house; place it in a vault, safe deposit box or another place where it cannot be stolen or destroyed. The time, trouble and expense in preparing all this evidence will pay off well in the event you ever have to file a claim for loss or damage to property.

Page 1

Application
for Registration of a Claim to Copyright
in a photograph

FORM J

REGISTRATION NO.

CLASS

J

DO NOT WRITE HERE
JFO   JF   JP   JU

Instructions: Make sure that all applicable spaces have been completed before you submit the form. The application must be **SIGNED** at line 9. For published works the application should not be submitted until after the date of publication given in line 4 (a), and should state the facts which existed on that date. For further information, see page 4.

Pages 1 and 2 should be typewritten or printed with pen and ink. Pages 3 and 4 should contain exactly the same information as pages 1 and 2, but may be carbon copies.

Mail all pages of the application to the Register of Copyrights, Library of Congress, Washington, D.C. 20559, together with:

(a) If unpublished, one complete copy of the work and the registration fee of $6.

(b) If published, two copies of the best edition of the work and the registration fee of $6.

Make your remittance payable to the Register of Copyrights.

1. Copyright Claimant(s) and Address(es): Give the name(s) and address(es) of the copyright owner(s). For published works the name(s) should ordinarily be the same as in the notice of copyright on the copies deposited. If initials are used in the notice, the name should be the same as appears elsewhere on the copies.

Name ....

Address ....

Name ....

Address ....

2. Title of Photograph: ....
(Give the title as it appears on the copies; each copy deposited should bear an identifying title, which may be descriptive)

....

3. Author: Citizenship and domicile information must be given. Where a work was made for hire, the employer is the author. The citizenship of organizations formed under U.S. Federal or State law should be stated as U.S.A.

If the copyright claim is based on new matter (see line 5) give information about the author of the new matter.

Name .... Citizenship ....
(Name of country)

Domiciled in U.S.A. Yes ...... No ...... Address ....

▶▶ **NOTE:** | Leave all spaces of line 4 blank unless your work has been PUBLISHED. | ◀◀

4. (a) Date of Publication: Give the complete date when copies of this particular photograph were first placed on sale, sold, or publicly distributed. The date when the photograph was made or the date when copies were reproduced should not be confused with the date of publication. NOTE: The full date (month, day, and year) must be given.

....
(Month)   (Day)   (Year)

(b) Place of Publication: Give the name of the country in which this particular photograph was first published.

....

▶▶ **NOTE:** | Leave all spaces of line 5 blank unless the instructions below apply to your work. | ◀◀

5. Previous Registration or Publication: If a claim to copyright in any substantial part of this work was previously registered in the U.S. Copyright Office in unpublished form, or if a substantial part of the work was previously published anywhere, give requested information.

Was work previously registered? Yes ...... No ...... Date of registration .... Registration number ....

Was work previously published? Yes ...... No ...... Date of publication .... Registration number ....

Is there any substantial **NEW MATTER** in this version? Yes ...... No ...... If your answer is "Yes," give a brief general statement of the nature of the **NEW MATTER** in this version. (New matter may consist of compilation, abridgment, editorial revision, and the like, as well as additional pictorial material.)

....

EXAMINER

Complete all applicable spaces on next page

6. If registration fee is to be charged to a deposit account established in the Copyright Office, give name of account:

----

7. Name and address of person or organization to whom correspondence or refund, if any, should be sent:

Name _____ Address _____

8. Send certificate to:

(Type or
print   Name _____
name and
address) Address _____
                                        (Number and street)
          _____
                    (City)   (State)   (ZIP code)

9. Certification:

(Application   I CERTIFY that the statements made by me in this application are correct to the
not acceptable   best of my knowledge.
unless signed)   _____
                         (Signature of copyright claimant or duly authorized agent)

Application Forms

Copies of the following forms will be supplied by the Copyright Office without charge upon request:

Class A	Form A—Published book manufactured in the United States of America.
Class A or B	Form A–B Foreign—Book or periodical manufactured outside the United States of America (except works subject to the ad interim provisions of the copyright law).
	Form A–B Ad Interim—Book or periodical in the English language manufactured and first published outside the United States of America.
Class B	Form B—Periodical manufactured in the United States of America.
	Form BB—Contribution to a periodical manufactured in the United States of America.
Class C	Form C—Lecture or similar production prepared for oral delivery.
Class D	Form D—Dramatic or dramatico-musical composition.
Class E	Form E—Musical composition the author of which is a citizen or domiciliary of the United States of America or which was first published in the United States of America.
	Form E Foreign—Musical composition the author of which is not a citizen or domiciliary of the United States of America and which was not first published in the United States of America.
Class F	Form F—Map.
Class G	Form G—Work of art or a model or design for a work of art.
Class H	Form H—Reproduction of a work of art.
Class I	Form I—Drawing or plastic work of a scientific or technical character.
Class J	Form J—Photograph.
Class K	Form K—Print or pictorial illustration.
	Form KK—Print or label used for an article of merchandise.
Class L or M	Form L–M—Motion picture.
Class N	Form N—Sound recording.
•	Form R—Renewal copyright.
•	Form U—Notice of use of copyrighted music on mechanical instruments.

FOR COPYRIGHT OFFICE USE ONLY	
Application received	
One copy received	
Two copies received	
Fee received	
Renewal	

Page 3

Certificate
Registration of a Claim to Copyright
in a photograph

FORM J

REGISTRATION NO.

CLASS

J

DO NOT WRITE HERE

This Is To Certify that the statements set forth on this certificate have been made a part of the records of the Copyright Office. In witness whereof the seal of the Copyright Office is hereto affixed.

Register of Copyrights
United States of America

1. Copyright Claimant(s) and Address(es):

Name ....

Address ....

Name ....

Address ....

2. Title of Photograph: ....
(Title of photograph as it appears on the copies)

....

3. Author:

Name .... Citizenship ....
(Name of country)

Domiciled in U.S.A. Yes ..... No ..... Address ....

4. (a) Date of Publication:

....
(Month)   (Day)   (Year)

(b) Place of Publication:

....
(Name of country)

5. Previous Registration or Publication:

Was work previously registered? Yes ..... No ..... Date of registration .... Registration number ....

Was work previously published? Yes ..... No ..... Date of publication .... Registration number ....

Is there any substantial **NEW MATTER** in this version? Yes ...... No ...... If your answer is "Yes," give a brief general statement of the nature of the **NEW MATTER** in this version.

....

....

EXAMINER

Complete all applicable spaces on next page

6. Deposit account:

---

7. Send correspondence to:

Name _____ Address_____

8. Send certificate to:

(Type or
print   Name _____
name and
address)   Address _____
                                        (Number and street)

                _____
                    (City)   (State)   (ZIP code)

Information concerning copyright in photographs

When to Use Form J. Form J is appropriate for unpublished and published photographs.

What Is a "Photograph"? This category (Class J) includes photographic prints and filmstrips, slide films, and individual slides.

—*Reproductions.* Reproductions of photographs prepared by photolithography and other mechanical processes are generally regarded as "prints" rather than "photographs" and, when published, should be submitted for registration on Form K.

—*Contributions to Periodicals.* When a photograph is first published with a separate copyright notice in a magazine or newspaper, it is regarded as a "contribution to a periodical," registrable on Form BB.

Duration of Copyright. Statutory copyright begins on the date the work was first published, or, if the work was registered for copyright in unpublished form, copyright begins on the date of registration. In either case, copyright lasts for 28 years, and may be renewed for a second 28-year term.

Unpublished photographs

How to Register a Claim. To obtain copyright registration, mail to the Register of Copyrights, Library of Congress, Washington, D.C. 20559, one complete copy of the photograph, an application on Form J, properly completed and signed, and a fee of $6. Deposits are not returned, so do not send your only copy.

Procedure to Follow if Work Is Later Published. If the photograph is later reproduced in copies and published, it is necessary to make a second registration, following the procedure outlined below. To maintain copyright protection, all copies of the published edition must contain a copyright notice in the required form and position.

Published photographs

What Is "Publication"? Publication, generally, means the sale, placing on sale, or public distribution of copies. Unrestricted public exhibition of a photograph may also constitute publication.

How to Secure Copyright in a Published Photograph:
1. *Produce copies with copyright notice.*
2. *Publish the work.*
3. *Register the copyright claim,* following the instructions on page 1 of this form.

The Copyright Notice. In order to secure copyright protection in a published work, it is important that all copies contain the statutory copyright notice. The notice should appear on the photograph itself, or, if the work is a collection of photographs in book form, on the title page or verso thereof. It should ordinarily consist of the word "Copyright," the ab-

breviation "Copr.," or the symbol ©, accompanied by the name of the copyright owner. The year date of publication may be included in the notice, but normally it is not required unless the work could also be regarded as a "book."

—*Alternative Form of Notice.* As an alternative, the notice for photographs may consist of the symbol ©, accompanied by the initials, monogram, mark, or symbol of the copyright owner, provided the owner's name appears on some accessible part of the copies.

—*Universal Copyright Convention Notice.* Use of the symbol © with the name of the copyright owner and the year date of publication may result in securing copyright in countries which are parties to the Universal Copyright Convention. Example: © John Doe 1976.

NOTE: If copies are published without the required notice, the right to secure copyright is lost and cannot be restored.

FOR COPYRIGHT OFFICE USE ONLY	
Application received	
One copy received	
Two copies received	
Fee received	

Citations

Chapter I: Taking the Picture

1. R.K.O. Midwest Corp. v. Berline, 51 Ohio App. 85, 199 N.E. 604 (1935)
2. N.Y. State Penal Law, Sec. 244
2a. Galella v. Onassis, 487 F.2d 986
2b. Le Mistral v. Columbia Broadcasting System, N.Y. Sup. Ct., N.Y. L.J. 6/7/76
3. Title 18, United States Code, Sec. 474
4. Title 18, United States Code, Sec. 504
5. Public Law 79, 82d Congress, approved July 16, 1951
6. E.g. N.Y. State Penal Law, Sec. 887
7. Title 18, United States Code, Sec. 504
8. Title 50, United States Code, Sec. 45 (repealed June 25, 1948), relating to photographs of defensive installations, is covered by Sections 795-797 of Title 18
9. Title 18, United States Code, Sec. 137
10. Title 49, United States Code, Sec. 121
11. Reported in Editor & Publisher, April 17, 1954
12. Ibid.
13. See Editor & Publisher, December 28, 1963, p. 9

Chapter II: Right of Privacy

1. It is generally settled that only living persons have a right of privacy. See, e.g., Wyatt v. Hill's Portrait Studio, 128 N.Y.S. 247 (1911)
2. 4 Harvard Law Review 193
3. In Manola v. Stevens & Myers, N.Y. Supreme Court, reported in The New York Times, June 15, 18, 21 (1890), where an actress had been photographed surreptitiously while performing in tights, the court enjoined publication of the photographs.
4. Roberson v. Rochester Folding Box Co., 171 N.Y. 538 (1902)
5. 15 Utah Rev. Stat., Secs. 103-4-7
6. Va. Code Title 8 Sec. 650 (1950)

7. Wisc. Stat. C. 348 Sec. 412 (1951)
8. See Proper on Torts
9. Lahiri v. Daily Mirror, 162 Misc. 776, 295 N.Y.S. 382 (1937)
10. Hofstadter, Development of the Right of Privacy in New York (1954)
11. Lahiri v. Daily Mirror, 162 Misc. 776, 295 N.Y.S. 382 (1937)
12. Koussevitzky v. Allen, Towne and Heath, 188 Misc. 479, aff'd 272 App. Div. 759 (1948)
13. Riddle v. MacFadden, 101 N.Y.S. 606 (1906), aff'd 201 N.Y. 215 (1911)
14. Booth v. Curtis Publishing Company, 15 A.D. 2d 343, 223 N.Y.S. 2d 737, aff'd 11 N.Y. 2d 907, 182 N.E. 2d 812, 228 N.Y.S. 2d 468 (1962)
15. Flores v. Mosler Safe Company, 7 N.Y. 2d 276, 196 N.Y.S. 2d 975 (1959)
16. Gautier v. Pro Football, Inc., 340 N.Y. 254 (1952)
16a. Rand v. Hearst Corp., 298 N.Y.S. 2d 405
16b. Pagan v. New York Herald Tribune, 32 A.D. 2d 341, 301 N.Y.S. 2d 120, aff'd 26 N.Y. 2d 941
16c. Porter v. New West Magazine (N.Y. L.J. 5/18/76)
17. Sutton v. Hearst Corp., 277 App. Div. 155 (1950)
18. See Leverton v. Curtis Publishing Co., 192 F. 2d 974 (3rd Cir. 1951)
19. Sweenek v. Pathe News Inc., 16 F. Supp. 746 (D.C. N.Y. 1936)
20. Humiston v. Universal Film Mfg. Co., 189 App. Div. 467 (1919)
21. Jenkins v. Dell Publishing Co., 251 F. 2d 487 (C.A. Pa. 1958)
21a. Time Inc. v. Hill, 385 U.S. 374
21b. Wojtowicz v. Delacorte Press, N.Y. Sup. Ct., N.Y.L.J. 8/26/76
22. Sidis v. F-R Pub. Corp., 113 F. 2d 806 (2d Cir. 1940) cert. den. 61 S.Ct. 393 (1940)
23. Wilson v. Brown, 189 Misc. 79 (1947)
24. Haelan Labs v. Topps Chewing Gum, 202 F. 2d 866 (1952) cert. den. 346 U.S. 816
24a. Spahn v. Messner, 18 N.Y. 2d 328, reargued 21 N.Y. 2d 124, appeal dismissed, 393 U.S. 1046
24b. Estate of Ernest Hemingway v. Random House Inc., 23 N.Y. 2d 341
24c. Rosemont Enterprises Inc. v. Random House Inc. & John Keats, 58 Misc. 2d 1
25. See Nimmer, The Right of Publicity, 1954, 19 Law & Contemp. Prob. 203
25a. Bell v. Birmingham Broadcasting Co., 96 So. 2d 263 (Ala. 1957)
25b. Paulsen v. Personality Posters Inc., N.Y. Sup. Ct., 299 N.Y.S. 2d 501
26. Time Inc. v. Firestone, 96 Sup. Ct. 957
27. Lahiri v. Daily Mirror, 162 Misc. 776, 882 (1937)
28. Callas v. Whisper, 101 N.Y.S. 2d 532 (1951), 278 App. Div. 964, aff'd 303 N.Y. 759
28a. Oma v. Hillman Periodicals Inc., 281 App. Div. 240, 118 N.Y.S. 2d 720
28b. Dallesandro v. Henry Holt & Co., 4 A.D. 2d 470, 166 N.Y.S. 2d 805 (1957)

28c. Murray v. N.Y. Magazine Co. (App. Div., N.Y. Sup. Ct., N.Y.L.J. 7/16/70)
29. Leverton v. Curtis Pub. Co., 192 F. 2d 974 (3rd Cir. 1951)
30. Gill v. Curtis Pub. Co., 239 P. 2d 630 (Cal. 1952)
31. See, e.g. Kelly v. Johnson Pub. Co., 325 P. 2d 659 (Cal. App. 1959)
31a. N.Y. Times Co. v. Sullivan, 376 U.S. 254
31b. Bavarian Motor v. Manchester, 61 Misc. 2d 309
32. See Footnote 1, also annotation in 14 A.L.R. 2d 757n.
33. Lawrence v. Ylla, 184 Misc. 807
34. Ibid.
35. Miller v. Madison Square Garden, 176 Misc. 714, 28 N.Y.S. 2d 811 (1941). There was a decision in New York that a gratuitous consent could be revoked at any time, but it is not expected that the courts would reach such a result where the photographer has taken action in reliance upon the gratuitous consent.
36. Buscelle v. Conde Nast Pub., 173 Misc. 674, 19 N.Y.S. 2d 129 (1940)
37. Sidney v. A. S. Beck Shoe Corp., 153 Misc. 166, 274 N.Y.S. 559 (1934)
38. Russel v. Marboro Books, 18 Misc. 2d 166, 183 N.Y.S. 2d 8 (1959)
39. Carlson v. Hillman Periodicals Inc., 3 A.D. 2d 987, 163 N.Y.S. 2d 21 (1957) reversing 157 N.Y.S. 2d 88
39a. Leslie v. Milky Way Productions, N.Y. Sup. Ct., N.Y.L.J. 8/12/76

Chapter III: Who Owns the Picture

1. White Studio Inc. v. Dreyfoos, 156 App. Div. 762 (N.Y.) (1913); Lumiere v. Robertson-Cole Distributing Corp., 280 Fed. 550 (2d Cir.), cert. den. 259 U.S. 583 (1922)
2. Colten v. Jacques Marchais, Inc., 61 N.Y.S. 2d 269 (N.Y.) (1946)
3. Hochstadter v. H. Tarr, Inc., 68 N.Y.S. 2d 762 (1947)
4. Avedon v. Exstein, 141 F. Supp. 278 (S.D.N.Y. 1956)
5. See note in Harvard Law Review, January, 1957, for an opinion that the court should have allowed evidence of trade usage to be introduced.
6. Press Publishing Co. v. Falk, 59 Fed. 324 (1894)
7. Thayer v. Worcester Post Co., 284 Mass. 160 (1933)
8. Young v. J. J. Hickerson, Inc., 159 N.Y.S. 2d 612, rev'd N.Y.L.J., Sept. 12, 1957 (App. Term)
9. Lawrence v. Ylla, 184 Misc. 807 (N.Y.)
10. Ibid.
11. Bakacs v. McGraw-Hill Inc., N.Y. Sup. Ct., N.Y.L.J. 4/1/76

Chapter IV: Loss of and Damage to Film

1. 228 N.Y.S. 2d 330
2. 12 N.Y. 2d 301, 239 N.Y.S. 2d 337, 189 N.E. 2d 693
3. Goor v. Navilio, 177 Misc. 970 (N.Y. 1941)

4. Nathan v. Fotoshop, 5th Dist. Mun. Ct. Man., N.Y. (1951)
5. Lake v. Railway Express Agency, 98 N.Y.S. 2d 202, 227 App. Div. 853 (1950)
6. Wamsley v. Atlas Steamship Co., 50 App. Div. 199 (N.Y. 1951)
7. Animals Enterprises Inc. v. Fabulous Forgeries Ltd. (N.Y. Sup. Ct., N.Y.L.J. 4/1/76)

Chapter V: The Nude in Photography and the Law of Obscenity

1. Title 18, United States Code, Sec. 334
2. N.Y. State Penal Law, Sec. 235.—235.22
3. N.Y. State Penal Law, Sec. 235.21
4. Kingsley Pictures Corp. v. Regents, 360 U.S. 684 (1959)
5. Commercial Pictures Corp. v. Regents, 346 U.S. 587 (1954)
6. Superior Films, Inc. v. Dep't of Education, 346 U.S. 587 (1954)
7. Gelling v. Texas, 343 U.S. 960 K (1952)
8. 354 U.S. 476 (1957); See also Alberts v. California, 354 U.S. 476 (1957)
9. 370 U.S. 478
10. See, e.g., Peiple v. Richmond County News, Inc., 9 N.Y. 2d 578 (1961)
11. People v. Finkelstein, 114 N.Y.S. 2d 810 (1952)
12. People v. Gonzales, 107 N.Y.S. 2d 968 (1951)
13. People v. Rosenzweig, 107 N.Y.S. 2d 968 (1951)
14. People v. Finkelstein, 107 N.Y.S. 968 (1951)
15. Jacobellis v. State of Ohio, 378 U.S. 184 (1964)
16. People v. Stabile, 296 N.Y.S. 2d 815
17. Cohen v. Carroll, N.Y.C. Crim. Ct., April 1970
18. Hosey v. City of Jackson, 309 F. Supp. 527
19. McGrew v. City of Jackson, 307 F. Supp. 754
20. Ratner v. Widdle, 307 F. Supp. 471
21. People v. Steinberg, 304 N.Y.S. 2d 858
22. U.S. v. Wild, 422 F. 2d 34
23. People v. Galbud Theatres Inc., N.Y.C. Crim. Ct., N.Y.L.J. 3/24/76

Chapter VI: Copyright

1. 13 World Book Encyclopedia 5582 (1938 ed.)
2. 38th Cong., 2d Sess., Ch. 126. See Copyright Enactments, Copyright Office, Bull. No. 3, rev.) p. 34
3. Although state protection for unpublished works is sometimes based on statute (e.g., Calif. Civil Code, Sec. 980(a), it is nevertheless referred to by general usage as "common-law copyright." The term "statutory copyright," according to accepted usage, refers to the federal Copyright Act, 17 U.S.C. 1 et seq. See Nimmer on Copyright 31, fn. (1964)

4. 376 U.S. 225 (1964)
5. See Capitol Records, Inc. v. Greatest Records, Inc., 142 U.S.P.Q. 109 (Sup. N.Y. Co., 1964); Columbia Broadcasting System, Inc. v. Documentaries Unlimited, Inc., 42 Misc. 2d 723 (1964); Flamingo Telefilm Sales, Inc. v. United Artists Corp., 141 U.S.P.Q. 461 (Sup., N.Y. Co., 1964)
6. Compco Corp. v. Day-Brite Lighting Co., 376 234 (1964), decided together with Sears Roebuck & Co. v. Stiffel Co., 376 U.S. 225, on the basis of the same rule of law, also involved a lamp. But see Jacobs v. Robitale, 406 F. Supp. 1145 and Vogue Ring Creations Inc. v. Hardman, 410 F. Supp. 609, which follow the Sears-Compco rule but indicate its limitations.
7. 17 U.S.C. § 2
8. Lumiere v. Pathe Exchange Inc., 275 Fed. 428
9. Washingtonian Publishing Co. v. Pearson, 306 U.S. 30 (1939)
10. Where the publisher acquires only limited reproduction rights, he often requires a specific consent to secure copyright in his name as part of the contract of purchase. This is one way to show, if necessary, that the publisher's general copyright notice in his magazine or book covered the particular photograph, thus preserving the copyright for the photographer.
11. See American Visuals Corporation v. Holland, 239 F. 2d 740 (2d Cir. 1956)
12. Gross v. Seligman, 212 F. 930 (1914)
12a. Tennessee Fabricating Co. v. Moultrie Mfg. Co., 421 F. 2d 279
13. Bolton v. Aldin, 56 L.J.B. 120 (1895)

Chapter VII: Libel by Photograph

1. Burton v. Crowell Publishing Co., 81 Fed. 154 (2d Cir. 1936)
2. This is usually accomplished by statute. See N.Y. State Penal Law Sec. 1342
3. Van Wiginton v. Pulitzer Pub. Co., 218 Fed. 795 (8th Cir. 1914)
4. Sydney v. MacFadden News Publishing Corp., 242 N.Y. 208 (1926)
5. Zbyszko v. N.Y. American, 239 N.Y.S. 411 (1930)
6. Reported in Editor & Publisher, Aug. 1, 1953, p. 40
7. Jackson v. Consumers Publications, Inc., 11 N.Y.S. 2d 462 (1932)
8. Meyers v. Afro-American Pub. Co., Inc., 5 N.Y.S. 2d 223 (1938)
8a. St. John v. N. Y. Times Co., N.Y. Sup. Ct., N.Y.L.J. 8/10/66
8b. Freemen v. Columbia Broadcasting System, N.Y. Sup. Ct., N.Y.L.J. 11/3/75
9. Peck v. Tribune Co., 214 U.S. 185 (1909)
10. See Liccione v. Collier, 117 N.Y.S. 639 (1909). The trial court was reversed on other grounds
11. Beck v. N.Y. Times, N.Y. Civ. Ct., N.Y.L.J. 2/2/76

Chapter VIII: Photographs as Evidence

1. Cowley v. People, 83 N.Y. 464 (1881)
2. Alberti v. New York L.E. & W.R.R. Co., 118 N.Y. 77 (1889)
3. Dresch v. Elliott, 137 App. Div. 252 (N.Y.) (1914)
4. Fearon v. New York Life Ins. Co., 162 App. Div. 560 (N.Y.) (1914)
5. Gibson v. Gunn, 206 App. Div. 464 (N.Y.) (1923)
6. Cirello v. Metropolitan Express Co., 88 N.Y.S. 932 (1904)
7. Cozzens v. Higgins, 3 Keyes 206, 33 How. Pr. 436 (N.Y.) (1886)
8. Boyarsky v. G. A. Zimmerman Corp., 240 App. Div. 361 (N.Y.) (1934)

Chapter IX: Photography—Business, Art or Profession

1. City of New Orleans v. Robira, 42 La. Ann. 1098 (1890)
2. Story v. Walker, 11 Lea 515 (Tenn.) (1883)
3. Cecil v. Inland Rev. Com., 36 Times Law Reports 164 (1919)
4. People v. Cross and Brown Co., 232 App. Div. 587, 251 N.Y.S. 138 (1931)
5. People ex rel Tower v. State Tax Com., 282 N.Y. 407 (1940)
6. Buehman v. Bechtel, 114 P. 2nd 227 (Arizona)
7. Territory v. Kraft, 33 Hawaii 397 (1935)
8. Wright v. Wiles, 173 Tenn. 334 (1938)
9. Schlesinger v. City of Atlanta, 161 Ga. 148 (1925)
10. State v. Cromwell, 9 N. Car. 2nd 914 (1943)

Index

Model Release Form A

In consideration of my engagement as model, upon the terms herein-after stated, I hereby give X, his legal representatives and assigns, those for whom X is acting, and those acting with his authority or permission, the absolute right and permission to copyright and/or use, re-use and/or publish, and/or republish photographic portraits or pictures of me or in which I may be included, in whole or in part, or composite or distorted in character or form, without restriction as to changes or alterations from time to time, in conjunction with my own or a fictitious name, or reproductions thereof in color or otherwise made through any media at his studios or elsewhere for art, advertising, trade, or any other purpose whatsoever.

I also consent to the use of any printed matter in conjunction therewith.

I hereby waive any right that I may have to inspect and/or appprove the finished product or products or the advertising copy or printed matter that may be used in connection therewith or the use to which it may be applied.

I hereby release, discharge, and agree to save harmless X, his legal representatives or assigns, and all persons acting under his permission or authority or those for whom he is acting, from any liability by virtue of any blurring, distortion, alteration, optical illusion, or use in composite form, whether intentional or otherwise, that may occur or be produced in the taking of said picture or in any subsequent processing thereof, as well as any publication thereof even though it may subject me to ridicule, scandal, reproach, scorn and indignity.

I hereby warrant that I am of full age and have every right to contract in my own name in the above regard. I state further that I have read the above authorization, release and agreement, prior to its execution, and that I am fully familiar with the contents thereof.

Date ....

Name .... (L.S.)

Witness ....

Address ....

Model Release Form B

For good and valuable consideration, the receipt of which is hereby acknowledged, I hereby consent that the photographs of me taken by John Doe, proofs of which are hereto attached, or any reproduction of the same, may be used by John Doe or his assigns or licensees for the purpose of illustration, advertising, trade, or publication in any manner.

Signed ....

Address ....

Date ....

Model Release Form C

I, (we) ....being of legal age hereby consent and authorize (client name), its successors, legal representatives and assigns, and the ABC Agency, Inc., ... New York, N.Y., its successors, legal representatives and assigns, to use and reproduce my name and photograph (or photographs) taken by .... on (date) and circulate the same for any and all purposes, including publication and advertising of every description. Receipt of full consideration of $............................. where acknowledged and no further claim of any kind will be made by me. No representations have been made to me.

....

(Name)

....

(Address)

Model Release Form D

I hereby affirm that I am the parent (guardian) of (name) and for value received and without further consideration I hereby irrevocably consent that each of the photographs which have been taken of him (her) by (name of photographer) and/or his (her) assigns may be used for advertising, trade, illustration, or publication in any manner.

....
(Name of parent or guardian)

....
(date)

Model Release Form E

Date ....

Place ....

I hereby consent to the use by you, or by anyone you authorize, for the purpose of advertising or trade, of my name and/or a portrait, picture or photograph of me, or any reproduction of same in any form.

Name ....

73

DATE DUE

Brynoff B reserve APR 25 1990			
DEC 1 2 1994			